THIS TOO SHALL PASS

Keeping Faith During Tough Times

MARGARET ANNE HUFFMAN

ANNE BROYLES

JUNE EATON

LYNN JAMES

BARBARA ROBERTS PINE

PUBLICATIONS INTERNATIONAL, LTD.

Margaret Anne Huffman is an award-wining journalist and former family/lifestyle editor of *The Shelbyville News*. She has written and contributed to eighteen books, including *Simple Prayers & Blessings, A Moment With God for Mothers*, and *Through the Valley: Prayers for Violent Times*.

Anne Broyles is a co-pastor and leads retreats throughout the country on a variety of family and women's spirituality topics. She is the author of many articles and books, including *Journaling: A Spirit Journey, Meeting God Through Worship,* and *Growing Together in Love: God Known Through Family Life*.

June Eaton is a teacher and freelance writer with an M.A. from Northwestern University. Her published work includes Sunday school curriculum, stories and articles in more than 50 Christian publications, and contributions to eight books.

Rev. Lynn James, L.C.P.C., is an ordained minister and co-pastor with a M.Div. from Christian Theological Seminary. In addition, she is a licensed clinical counselor in private practice, specializing in work with survivors of interpersonal violence.

Barbara Roberts Pine is an author and speaker who holds an M.A. in Theology from Fuller Theological Seminary. She has lectured at religious retreats and leadership seminars, and her published writing includes the book *Life With a Capital "L."*

Cover photo: Nicholas Parfitt/Tony Stone Images

Louis Weber, C.E.O.
Publications International, Ltd.
7373 North Cicero Avenue
Lincolnwood, Illinois 60646

Manufactured in U.S.A.

8 7 6 5 4 3 2 1

ISBN: 0-7853-2954-4

CONTENTS

INTRODUCTION

In a popular self-help book, the author describes his reaction to the devastating illness and eventual death of his young son. He rages at the unfairness of the situation and expresses his disbelief that this could happen to him—a good person and a man of God. He concludes that bad things do happen to good people.

Illness, death, broken relationships, and worldly setbacks occur in the life of every human being. When suffering invades your world, it's a natural reaction to experience anger and confusion. You may feel isolated—far removed from reality—and unprepared to deal rationally with the great, dark cloud that has suddenly descended upon you.

This Too Shall Pass is a book for just such times. In its pages you will meet people who lead lives much like yours and who have suffered trauma and tragedy. You can read their stories, learn how they have coped, and apply their wisdom to your own situation. You'll discover that things can get better.

The book is comprised of seven chapters of inspirational stories, quotes, prayers, and meditations, gathered from individuals who have gone through tough times and have emerged stronger as a result. Each of the first five chapters deals with a different aspect of trouble people are likely to encounter in their lives. The last two chapters discuss how to get on the path of general recovery from trauma and tragedy.

But the road to healing is not always a steady climb. The path can twist and turn; sometimes it is rocky; and sometimes you need to go backward to progress. But eventually the way does become clearer. Things do improve.

The collected wisdom in *This Too Shall Pass* can help you get to that place of hope and healing. Take time to read through these chapters, reflect on the stories and share them with others. In the process you will not only heal—you will also learn to adapt and even to grow through your experience.

Chapter 1:

WHEN LOSS SADDENS YOUR LIFE

Is there anything more painful than the death of a loved one—a precious parent, spouse, friend, child? When such a loss occurs, we feel the world should stop turning; all life should freeze in its tracks, just as time seems to have stopped for us. And yet, life goes on, despite our protestations. And, impossible though it seems at first, healing can and does take place. With honest grieving, understanding friends, and the passage of time, it becomes possible to cope and begin living for ourselves again. After all, it does not dishonor the dead to take care of the living, even as we treasure our memories of our lost ones.

In the following stories and thoughts, you will see just a few of the forms healing can take. With the help of God, good companions, and our own resources, life after loss is possible.

A Numbing Loss

For Larry and Joni, battling their daughter's lymphoma meant watching her endure endless rounds of chemotherapy, radiation, and even a bone marrow transplant. Martha had seemed so strong, they always believed there was hope. But after a five-and-a-half-year battle with the disease, she died at age 35.

"Martha wasn't just my daughter," says Joni. "She was my best friend, and I miss her."

An accomplished violinist, Martha loved life. She had a positive attitude and a ready smile. Friends valued the twinkle in her eyes as much as they did the fragile beauty of her violin solos.

"People ask me how I could be so brave and accepting in the face of my daughter's death. I'm

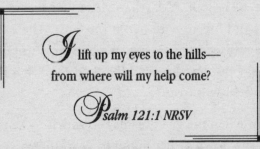

I lift up my eyes to the hills—
from where will my help come?

Psalm 121:1 NRSV

not. It is a numbing loss and I'm still working through it," explains Joni. "But as a mother you don't want to see your children sick. If Martha had lived any longer, she would have been sick. Very sick. Her father and I were torn between wanting to have her with us as long as possible yet not wanting to see her suffer any more."

A week before her death Martha was still remodeling her condo. Then the drugs stopped working. Suddenly she had no resistance left and the disease overtook her.

Martha once made a list of ways to overcome her illness: "1. Think positive; 2. Make plans; 3. Pray; 4. Be with people; 5. Laugh and cry; 6. Do things for others; 7. Know what's going on and be part of decisions; 8. List questions; 9. Live life—don't stop."

"That will show you what kind of person she was," says Joni. "Martha's sister, her friend Lisa, and I were with her at the end," she adds. "She refused life support. We had time to talk and say our good-byes. I thanked God that her long fight was over."

Often when the grief seems too much to bear, Joni sits down at her piano to work her way through the pain. She pounds furiously on the keys, prayers and tears mingling with the music, until her emotions are spent.

She also relies on the support of family and friends. There is always someone nearby to lean on. Prayers for Martha and the family have even flooded the Internet.

The grieving mother admits she's had lots of nightmares about her daughter's final day, replaying it again and again in her dreams. "For weeks," she recalls, "I'd wake up with disturbed thoughts. Then one night when I awoke, I was at peace. I thought: Jesus suffered. If God could accept his suffering and watch his child die, then I could, too."

. . . in all human sorrows nothing gives comfort but love and faith.

LEO TOLSTOY, *ANNA KARENINA*

SOME THINGS CANNOT BE STOLEN

Hear Augustine's cry:
   "I wondered that my friend should die
   And I remain alive,
      For I was the second half of his soul."
At the death of my dear friend.
Loss ripped at my heart,
   Struggling to steal my part of her soul.
    I'll not be robbed, our bond stays whole.
    I flatly refused to let her soul go.

From my heart I can say that a little boy led me to some great discoveries. God makes no mistakes. He graciously accomplished much in my life through Jeffrey's death that could never have taken place otherwise. Questions were raised that I might never have asked. Answers were found that I might never have sought.

FRAN SANDIN, *SEE YOU LATER JEFFREY*

CARRYING A LOAD

It's lonely, Lord, being left. The burden to carry
on alone bends me over like a willow in the
wind. I feel you scoot closer; thank you.

Felicity of Grief!—even Death being kind,
Reminding us how much we dared to love!

EDNA ST. VINCENT MILLAY

LEARNING TO MOVE ON

When Camille saw the blue Air Force van
drive up to her home at Bergstrom Air
Force base in Austin, Texas, she knew something was wrong.

Her husband, Ed, an Air Force major and a vet-
eran pilot of the Vietnam and Korean Wars,
was on a six-month tour of duty in Denmark,
helping the Danes to establish their air force.

His tour was just about over, and she had her passport ready so that she could join him on a furlough overseas. Her in-laws had come to town to care for their two children, ages 4 and 7.

As the commanding officer of the base, a chaplain, and the squadron nurse emerged from the vehicle, 7-year-old Jack also sensed trouble and cried out, "What's wrong with my daddy?"

Camille whisked the children off to their rooms and opened the door. "What is it?" she asked, trying to control the alarm in her voice. "Something's happened, hasn't it?"

Without a word, the colonel rushed in and put his arms around her. They stood locked in a tearful embrace for a long time before the details emerged.

The news of her husband's fatal air crash left her stunned, her world shattered. "But he's flown hundreds of missions in wartime. Why would he crash now?" she cried.

Her first concerns were for the children she'd have to care for all alone. Their daddy was never coming back. He'd never again play with them, bathe them, tell them stories, or tuck them into bed. The thought nearly over-whelmed her, but she quickly regained her poise and went to comfort them.

"When you have two small children to take care of, you can't waste time crying," Camille muses. "I had to make a life for them.

"My first thought was to get them as stable as I could. I knew immediately that I'd go back to the Chicago area to be among friends and family. It was a thing I had to do for the kids and for myself."

Camille's parents came to be with her, and an outpouring of love and support came to her through the men of the squadron and their wives, as well as friends and family. They did everything from washing the dirty dishes in her sink to finding a home for her to live in when she returned to Chicago.

Ed's best friend Bill, stationed in Nevada, was given a 30-day leave to help Camille with the mounds of paperwork that needed to be done. His advice to her was to leave the base as soon as possible in order to spare her from further heartbreak.

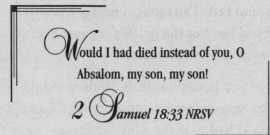

Would I had died instead of you, O Absalom, my son, my son!

2 *Samuel 18:33 NRSV*

"Relying on the help of others was such a comfort to me," she reflects. "Letting people do things for you is a help to them, too. It's a way for them to express their grief. With such an expression of love, even in the midst of 'the valley of the shadow of death,' I could truly say, 'My cup runneth over.'" (Psalm 23).

In the weeks that followed, occupied with moving and tending to legal matters, Camille says she was too busy to think, and she acknowledges that keeping busy was good therapy. It wasn't until a month later, when she landed in the hospital for thyroid surgery, that the loneliness began to sweep over her. "But I was confident that God wouldn't give me more sorrow than I could take," she claims, "and I was determined to resist feeling sorry for myself and to keep going forward."

Then in May, just three months after her husband's death, Bill, the friend who had helped her through the first weeks of her difficult time, died in a plane crash in Nevada.

Quickly, Camille hurried to the side of his wife to offer the kind of loving help she had received, by caring for the couple's two children. It was then that she learned another valuable lesson. Thinking of others, she found, kept her mind off her own troubles.

At the same time, she realized that death and tragedy would always be a part of life and she'd have to accept it and move on. This attitude of acceptance helped her in later years as she dealt with the death of her son in a hunting accident at age 16 and then her own bout with cancer.

"What helped me most in the months that followed my husband's death was being a part of a group of close-knit friends back in my home state. We did things for one another, got together for holidays, and went out for dinner every Friday. We were like an extended family. Friendship and companionship were important parts of my healing, and the children never lacked for loving relationships."

Today, many years later, Camille continues to express her appreciation for the help she received during her time of need, by helping others through their grief. One way she does this is by cooking and serving funeral luncheons for the bereaved people at her church. "I think it's important that we should help. It's the least we can do for those who are grieving. We can give them the time to be with friends and family around the table. It's the best kind of healing there is."

Praise be to the God and Father of our Lord Jesus Christ, the Father of compassion and the God of all comfort, who comforts us in all our troubles, so that we can comfort those in any trouble with the comfort we ourselves have received from God.

2 Corinthians 1:3–4 NIV

Sing the wondrous love of Jesus,
Sing his mercy and his grace;
In the mansions bright and blessed,
He'll prepare for us a place.

While we walk the pilgrim pathway,
Clouds will overspread the sky;
But when trav'ling days are over,
Not a shadow, not a sigh.

When we all get to heaven,
What a day of rejoicing that will be!
When we all see Jesus,
We'll sing and shout the victory.

ELIZA E. HEWITT, "WHEN WE
ALL GET TO HEAVEN"

ON A JOURNEY OF HEALING

Grief, O God of current and tides, is taking me
somewhere new. Feeling your guiding hand, I
will hold on and keep moving.

And now, dear brothers, I want you to know what happens to a Christian when he dies so that when it happens, you will not be full of sorrow, as those are who have no hope.

1 Thessalonians 4:13 TLB

In the depths of your grief you may have been struck by the absurdity, pointlessness, and meaninglessness of the death of your beloved. Now, without that person, you feel abandoned.... You ask, "Is there any meaning at all to this death...?"

You will search in vain for some "reason" that makes the death of your beloved seem fair, just, and understandable. However, God works after the fact of the death to bring meaning to your life.

WAYNE E. OATES, *YOUR PARTICULAR GRIEF*

HOW COULD THIS HAPPEN?

Karen and Jim had arrived at a happy time in their lives. Their son had graduated from high school, their daughter had married, and Jim had taken an early retirement from his stressful job at a local TV station. Now they were free to build their dream home in the Colorado mountains.

Their son Peter seemed eager to go with them and join in the adventure. An excellent student, he also planned on going to college out West. So the three of them packed up and moved. They rented a house at first, while they searched for just the right place to build. Two years later, amid the splendor of the snow-capped mountains, their well loved son put a bullet through his brain. He was 20 years old.

> Do not be afraid, little flock, for it is your Father's good pleasure to give you the kingdom.
>
> *Luke 12:32 NRSV*

The parents left Colorado and returned home, the wrenching grief too much to bear. When the people of their church offered little support, the hurt became even more overwhelming. "We felt accused," Karen says. "But we held on to our faith. We knew the Lord wasn't rejecting us."

At the funeral, people were awkward about expressing their condolences. Karen wanted to scream, "Don't tell me you know how I feel! You don't!"

She remembers how one friend came, put her arms around them, and simply cried with them. "That brought more comfort than any words," she remembers.

Being reunited with their daughter gave Jim and Karen comfort, and she needed them as much as they needed her. But the grief was too deep. Their lives remained frozen in time. Jim continued to be haunted by the circumstances of the death. Karen could still hear her husband's screams when he discovered their son's body.

Then followed a litany of "if onlys" and second guessing. "If only we had known... If only he'd told us what was bothering him... Why didn't we?... We could have... We should have...."

The refrain kept going round and round in their heads.

Jim and Karen could see they weren't going to get through this alone. They needed professional help and they knew it. The couple began a two-year odyssey, traveling from one grief counselor to the next across the country. They attended one therapy session after another, but Jim could not be consoled. It soon became apparent that he needed medical help for his deep depression.

"Sometimes all the talking in the world is not going to help," the doctor told Karen. "You can see where it only got you so far. Jim needs more than just talk." So Karen put him in the hospital for treatment.

Finally, with that added boost, both slowly began to heal.

In the end, their healing hinged on one phrase: "Don't blame yourself for what you cannot control."

What, then, should guard the gate?
How shall a man be great?
Through the dark days and long,
What power shall make him strong?
Wherein does courage lie,
Since all he loves must die?

When sorrow binds his hands,
Helpless the strong man stands.
One master only grief
Bows to, and that's belief—
Faith that he'll some day know
Why God hath willed it so!

EDGAR GUEST, "GRIEF'S ONLY MASTER"

FLOWERS FOR THE TABLE

We linger at the grave, O God, needing you to
lead us through this valley of fading bouquets
and crushing grief into the land of living. When
it's time, go with us to buy flowers for our
tables along with flowers for the graves we visit.

O God, O God, how long, how long? Why hast Thou forsaken me? Why can't I open my heart? Why is it closed, closed, closed? Why can't I feel my husband is alive instead of dead? In the cold tomb.

CLARISSA START, *WHEN YOU'RE A WIDOW*

BLESSINGS FROM MEMORY'S GARDEN

I sit in what once was and grieve what is lost forever. And yet words once heard float like mind-perfume, opening up a floodgate of memory, recalling the moments when those words were spoken. And I am comforted. Thank you, O God, for the gift of remembering.

Let Love clasp Grief lest both be drown'd...

ALFRED, LORD TENNYSON, "IN MEMORIAM"

KEEP IT SIMPLE

Left alone now, we drift aimlessly like untied balloons let loose to fly helter-skelter. Yet life goes on, decisions must be made. O God, help us make up minds that won't stay still. Give us good sense to put off until tomorrow what we shouldn't try today. Reassure us this is only temporary, a brief hesitation, not a giving up; hold up a mirror for us to see a once-again clear-eyed person.

It is always a tragic thing when a child dies. People have a tendency to call this an injustice on the part of God. However, God owes us nothing. If He gives our child ten years and then takes him away, we must be grateful for those ten years.

Also, I know how the Lord can use such happenings to accomplish a good purpose.

CORRIE TEN BOOM, *HE CARES, HE COMFORTS*

As you face death with all its impact on your feelings and your way of life, the greatest force for sustaining you and bringing meaning to the apparently meaningless, is your ability to see life not with physical preoccupations but in the light of the New Testament revelation.

EDGAR N. JACKSON, *WHEN SOMEONE DIES*

I will not leave you comfortless:
I will come to you.

Jesus, John 14:18 KJV

Grief melts away
Like snow in May,
As if there were no such cold thing.

GEORGE HERBERT, "THE FLOWER"

*August 1976 (one year after Sarah's death in
a car accident at 1 year old)*

Dear Sarah:
*... Even though our love stretches beyond any
grave, my life here is without you. You've
become the seed of a new beginning.... I still
cry for you... maybe that will always be
so.... I understand and accept that as part of
love. But can you see what I'm trying to say?
I'm saying goodbye...*

PAULA D'ARCY, *SONG FOR SARAH*

DOWN BUT NOT OUT

Like a toddler who falls more than he stands,
I'm pulling myself upright in the aftermath of
death. I know you as companion, God of mend-
ing hearts, and feel you steadying me. Thank
you for the gift of resilience. Lead me to others
who have hurt and gone on; I need to see how
it's done.

> When the cares of my heart are many,
> your consolations cheer my soul.
>
> *Psalm 94:19 NRSV*

AFTER THE RAIN

Life, once filled with sunlight and promise, has
been colored by loss to be all storm and
shadow. Use my tears, Lord, as the showers
needed to bring rainbows. Shine your love on
me as the sun; lift my eyes so I can see even the
smallest curves of hope in the lightening sky.

Speak low to me, my Saviour, low and sweet
From out the hallelujahs, sweet and low
Lest I should fear and fall, and miss Thee so
Who art not missed by any that entreat.
Speak to me as to Mary at thy feet!
And if no precious gums my hands bestow,
Let my tears drop like amber while I go

In reach of thy divinest voice complete
In humanest affection—thus, in sooth,
To lose the sense of losing . . .

ELIZABETH BARRETT BROWNING, "COMFORT"

*W*eeping may linger for the night,
but joy comes with the morning.

*P*salm 30:5 NRSV

TAKING STOCK

Help me grieve and go on . . . go on in new ways
you will reveal to me, Lord, as I make my faltering way as far as I can. Hold me while I
name and mourn all I have lost, weeping and
wailing like the abandoned child I feel I am.
Then, in time and with you to lean on, I can
focus on what I have left.

Think not thou canst sigh a sigh
And thy maker is not by;
Think not thou canst weep a tear
And thy maker is not near.

O! he gives to us his joy
That our grief he may destroy;
Till our grief is fled & gone
He doth sit by us and moan.

WILLIAM BLAKE, "ON ANOTHER'S SORROW"

*H*e leads me beside still waters; he
restores my soul.

*P*salm 23:2–3 NRSV

IN TIME

There will be tomorrows, and we'll be ready,
having spent today healing.

*Because my heart is sore, I have shut the door
of my heart to my fellows, and even to Thee.
But I sense that withdrawal and the effort to
dull my feelings is not the way toward healing.
Help me now to dare to open my being wide to
the balm of Thy loving Spirit, unafraid of any
depth or height or intensity of overflowing
emotion.*

PETER MARSHALL,
THE PRAYERS OF PETER MARSHALL

DADDY'S GIRL

On the day my father died, an ache developed deep inside of me and swelled like a balloon every time I thought of him. People said, "He lived a long life—he was 79." Not long enough for me. I was "daddy's girl."

Dad raised his family in one of the most difficult times in recent history—the Great Depression. I remember him as always being busy.

When he couldn't find employment, Dad made work for himself. He did household repairs and remodeling for the landlord in exchange for the rent. When Mom needed extensive dental work, he painted the dentist's house in lieu of payment. And he made things to sell: wooden shelves, sewing boxes, game boards, knick-knacks.

One year at Christmas he made me a beautiful dollhouse complete with curtains, wallpaper, and a row of green-dyed sponges for shrubbery. That's what it meant to be daddy's girl. It also meant thinking my father was the smartest, strongest, and wittiest person in the world.

It meant being able to face whatever the world threw at me because I knew that I was loved unconditionally.

It meant spending my entire life living up to a standard of excellence that he expected, but never demanded.

It meant always being provided for as a child, not having everything I wanted, but always having enough.

It meant living in a home that was always bright and freshly decorated and surrounded by a yard full of tulips and peony bushes.

It meant a house full of company every Saturday night, with lots of laughter and music.

It meant getting a college education when it wasn't popular for women to do so.

It meant, most of all, being able to count on him for the answers to life's most perplexing problems.

How could I cope with a loss like that? Part of my history had suddenly disappeared. All I could do now was remember and be thankful for all the good traits he instilled in me—determination, a strong work ethic, the will to excel, a love of words. And I could honor him by taking care of my mother, as he had done for so many years.

I would no longer have the benefit of Dad's physical presence or his wisdom. I would have to go out and find my own answers. But in my sadness I discovered I had another father, a heavenly Father, and he would give me all the help I would need.

I hold it true, whate'er befall;
  I feel it, when I sorrow most;
    'Tis better to have loved and lost
Than never to have loved at all.

ALFRED, LORD TENNYSON, "IN MEMORIAM"

FITTING PIECES TOGETHER

Remind me, Lord, that to cry, rage, sit dumbly, or chatter incessantly—whatever I need to get through these moments—is okay. Allowed to blaze, grief soon wears itself out and is no more than a beacon to follow into tomorrow.

Record my lament;
list my tears on your scroll—
are they not in your record?

Psalm 56:8 NIV

Chapter 2:

WHEN ALL IS NOT WELL

When illness strikes, the effects go beyond the physical suffering. Fear, despair, and terrible isolation arise as the illness prolongs itself. It feels natural to lash out at your failing body, medicine that does not help, and even at the God who allowed this terrible thing to happen to you. The fate of the patient's loved ones can be equally painful, as they stand by feeling helpless to be of any real assitance.

The people in this chapter have faced the burden of serious illness and found their own ways to triumph. The common elements of their victories seem to be finding their inner resources of strength and accepting help from God and from the loved ones who act as God's ministering hands in times of trouble.

SURVIVOR

My dad, a building tradesman, was strong, vigorous, and active, the "rock" on which our family relied. Even in retirement, he kept up a steady schedule of exercise, repairs to the house, gardening, and woodworking projects.

Then came diabetes, a wound that wouldn't heal, and the amputation of his left leg.

The family was in shock. To me, his daughter, the loss of that limb was like a death in the family, and I was in the first stage of the grieving process—denial.

"No!" I cried. "They can't do that to my father! God, where are you? Have you deserted him?"

But Dad took the news with a stoic, wait-and-see attitude. Throughout his hospital stay, he remained optimistic. He plunged into physical therapy with determination and joked about feeling pain in a leg that was no longer there.

Soon it was time to leave the protective womb of the hospital, and I sensed my father's courage faltering. I knew what was going through his mind. He and mom lived in a rural area where a car was a necessity. Mom took care of the cleaning, laundering, and cooking with expertise—but she couldn't drive. Dad had to chauffeur her everywhere. If he, too, were unable to drive, would the two of them be trapped in their home indefinitely, relying on neighbors and relatives for occasional rides?

We got into my car, and Dad sat grim-faced and silent all the way home from the hospital. I chattered nonstop, trying to fill the silence as he looked out the window toward an unknown future.

"Guess I won't be able to climb a ladder and fix the roof anymore," he observed. "Or roughhouse with the grandkids." He sighed.

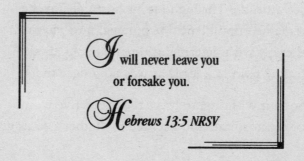

I will never leave you
or forsake you.
Hebrews 13:5 NRSV

As we approached the house, Dad started fidgeting restlessly. "Stop the car!" he shouted as we came to the end of the driveway. Reaching into the backseat, he grabbed his walker and pulled it out through the open door.

With his empty pantleg flapping in the breeze, he slowly made his way to the garage. Easing himself into his car, Dad turned on the engine and slowly backed the car out of the garage. He drove the car up and down the length of the driveway several times, then put it back in the garage.

He emerged with a satisfied smile. *I can still do that,* his expression seemed to say. *I still have some control over my life.* He wouldn't be dependent on someone else to drive. He wouldn't be housebound. And who knows what other things he could accomplish?

I was wrong. God had not deserted him.

There was hope after all. Who knew it would come in the form of an automobile.

Some other doctors and nurses came and stood looking down at me . . .

They told each other that something was wrong, because I didn't "respond" to their "tests" like other babies did. Poor souls! I could have told them that this, too, was part of the Plan. But they couldn't know that—they didn't have eyes to see You there beside me, or ears to hear Your voice.

DALE EVANS ROGERS, *ANGEL UNAWARE*, A BOOK INSPIRED BY HER DOWN SYNDROME CHILD

A BRIDGE TO THE YONDER VALLEY

The final healing, O God, is near, and my body is painfully ready. Help me think of this as a "birthing pain," for I'm in the process of becoming new. Deliver me onto that other shore newly born and healed from this life's travail. Hold my hand, for pain's waves are building into a sea strong enough for us to walk across at last.

CAN WE HELP EACH OTHER?

Time binds words, bones,
   And those who work together.
Time bends meanings, mountain spines, and
   daylight.
Time braids our calamity and joy,
   Melts together our many moods,
      Strains them and serves up to God the
      resulting libation;
         Sweet or sour—strong or weak.
Time will take us,
   From this measured dimension
      And deliver us to eternity.
         Blessed are those who help along the
         way.

Be strong and courageous; do not be
frightened or dismayed, for the Lord your God
is with you wherever you go.

Joshua 1:9 NRSV

An Illness of Memory

I chase after symptoms like a child playing tag.
Some days I forget what to do, O God, and
where I am, lost here on the dead-end road of
Alzheimer's. Stay with me on good days and
bad and the precarious ones in between; I feel
so alone, separated as I am even from myself.
You are the only constant in my perplexing life.

It Doesn't Get Any Better than This

Ray is a man of few words, but there's one
phrase he uses frequently: "It doesn't get
any better than this."

Nearly every activity he engages in—riding
horses in the Tetons, viewing glaciers from
Alaska's inner passage, sailing through the
Panama Canal, or listening to the Chicago Sym-
phony play Beethoven—elicits that comment.

Maybe that's because he is happy just to be
alive after surviving no less than four heart

bypass operations. The longest interval between his surgeries was eight years; the shortest, only one year.

"Is this my last chance for surgery?" he asked his doctor after his most recent hospitalization, knowing that each time a vein or artery must be harvested from some other part of his body.

"No, we have plenty of arteries left," the surgeon assured him.

Ray is a trim 63-year-old retired engineer, healthy in every way but one: In spite of a strict low-fat diet, a vigorous exercise regime, and a healthy lifestyle (he neither smokes nor drinks) his body manufactures excessive plaque that clogs the arteries to his heart. It has to do with the genes, he says. His father and uncle had similar heart problems.

He has been exercising and counting fat grams for nearly twenty years to compensate for the hand nature dealt him. Before his drastic lifestyle changes, he admits to eating 24-ounce steaks and all the eggs he wanted. "But now it's frustrating to do everything right and still have problems," Ray says.

The days and months following surgery are tough ones as he tries to overcome pain and discomfort and regain his strength. He notices a marked memory loss every time he undergoes the seven hours of anesthesia required for the surgery. "And each time it takes longer to recover," he adds. "Six weeks after the first operation, I was cutting wood for my sauna with a chain saw. This time it's taken much longer."

"Every time he has to go to the hospital for angioplasty or surgery, chest pains or fluid buildup, I want to cry and beat the floor," says his wife Lois. "My blood pressure just keeps going up."

"Between hospital stays, I live a fairly normal life—though I do have some restrictions," Ray explains. "For example, I'm not allowed to lift more than 35 pounds." And he has to take six prescribed medications a day.

In spite of his medical history, Ray refuses to act like an invalid. He walks 45 minutes a day, exercises, volunteers at the hospital, helps clear brush and burn fields at the local forest preserve, and goes on plenty of vacations.

> *S*uffering produces endurance, and endurance produces character, and character produces hope.
>
> *R*omans 5:3–4 NRSV

Recently, he and a group of other retirees repainted the interior of their church. A few winters ago he took part in a study at Yellowstone Park, spending full days on snowshoes, tracking wildlife in heavy snow and temperatures down to 30 degrees below zero. Before that, he joined an Earthwatch team in Puerto Rico, trapping, tagging, and studying the troublesome mongoose.

Each time he proposes one of these adventurous trips, Lois holds her breath, prays, then lets him go. She doesn't even want to think of what could happen out in the wild during a medical emergency.

Before each trip, he's had to undergo strenuous stress tests to prove his fitness. "Most of the time he's in better shape than I am," says his doctor. "He has incredible stamina. Ray could teach the class on cardiac rehab."

His friends say he's just plain stubborn, but Ray thinks it takes more than determination to survive what he's survived and still manage to enjoy life.

"It helps having a wife who's a nurse," he admits. "She takes good care of me. And my faith is also important. Talking to God and listening to him, especially before surgery, helps me feel good about the outcome."

"A sense of humor doesn't hurt, either," Lois says. "Last time in the ICU, he talked about trading in his 'bad genes' for Levi's or Wranglers. Imagine—joking at a time like that!"

Renounce all strength, but strength divine,
And peace shall be for ever thine.

Lincoln's Devotional

A LIFE-THREATENING RIDDLE

Is illness your will, Lord? I need answers, for I
want you to help me heal. But if you send
illness, how can I trust you to heal? Reassure me
that you will work everything out eventually.
And when that isn't possible, you are with me as
I suffer. Freed from fear I can get stronger as
your healing energy flows through me, restoring
me to my abundant life.

*When illness strikes, there are a number of
things which worry us.*

*. . . In all our anxieties, prayer helps. We can
pray for the recovery of the patient and for the
welfare of the rest of the family. We can pray
for added strength, a little more patience and
understanding, the ability to remain calm and
clear-thinking and to endure the personal
inconveniences.*

DONNA L. GLAZIER, *HEAVEN HELP ME*

. . . their little boy had contracted a brain disease that left him an invalid. He spent his entire life in bed, unable to speak, read, or use his hands creatively.

"Pastor, don't feel sorry for us because of Kenny," his parents told me. "People think he's a burden, but to us, he's a blessing from God. We've learned so much about God's grace in taking care of Kenny."

Warren Wiersbe, *Why Us? When Bad Things Happen to God's People*

Savvy Recovery

The outlook is promising, progress steady. Yet, O God, we're afraid to relax for fear illness will sneak up again. Guide us through these shaky days of recovery. Remind us that if we've done it once, we can outwit illness if it dares strike again. As veterans of this illness, we have the scars to prove it!

TESTING, TESTING

Scared as much of the tests as of their findings, I
shiver flimsily gowned and alone on this side of
a diagnosis. Closing my eyes and breathing
deeply, I feel God's warming presence around
my shoulders.

LIVING WITH IT

She first became aware that all was not well
with her body while on duty as a surgical
nurse. Linda was hanging up an X ray in the
operating room when she noticed its strange
appearance. The edges were fuzzy. She peered at
it again and couldn't seem to focus her eyes.

"Something is wrong in my brain," she told
another nurse. "I think I'm having a stroke."

Her coworker wouldn't let her drive home
alone. Instead, she sent Linda right to her doctor, who referred her to a neurologist.

In the following weeks Linda noticed a lack of
dexterity. She began dropping objects. "I'd pick

up a surgical instrument, and the next thing I knew, it was falling to the ground. When I tried to feed myself, the food would miss my mouth and go over my right shoulder."

The diagnosis was multiple sclerosis, a disease of the nerve sheaths in the brain and spinal cord, often marked by muscle tremor and paralysis.

"At first I was relieved that it wasn't a stroke," she says. "I kept telling myself that it was going to get better." But as the months went by, she could see this disease was going to be a formidable enemy.

Her two sons were just out of diapers, Linda recalls. "I'd get so tired at the end of the day, I'd just take them off to bed and read to them for hours."

Besides fatigue, other problems developed. She became very emotional, flying off the handle over the slightest incident.

"It was difficult to keep my marriage together. My husband became frustrated because he wasn't able to fulfill his lifelong dreams. He took a job in Germany." They were separated for a number of years before he died.

Though she tries to keep her spirits up, Linda admits to having some stress points. Financial security for a disabled single woman is one. Loss of independence is another. She says she's working on both, trying to plan ahead financially and using every means she can to remain independent for as long as possible.

The physical limitations are particularly difficult to deal with. She can't kneel and is unable to descend stairs with ease or to use an escalator. Walking is a challenge, but last year a new medication made it possible for her to discard her cane, so there's hope on the medical front.

A decline in Linda's physical abilities prompted a recent job change. "A surgical nurse needs energy and dexterity," she says. "I have neither." Her supervisor suggested a desk job, but MS is a use-it-or-lose-it disease. If she doesn't stay on her feet, she's afraid she won't walk at all. She had to settle for a position in outpatient surgery, preparing patients for surgery. "Of course, with shorter hours and less stress, the pay is lower, too."

Linda doesn't know how much longer she'll be able to drive, and that will create a problem getting to work. She knows she'll eventually go on disability, but until then, she keeps as active as her body will allow. That includes attending church, bible study classes, and social functions; serving on her church's calling ministry team; and swimming four times a week.

Her motto is to keep life simple. Her prayers, she says, are one continuous run-on sentence. "I dedicate myself to God, and in return He gives me strength and grace."

Linda believes a cheering section is a necessity for a person with a progressive disease. Her boys, now grown, are a great source of help and support, as are the nurses in the operating room where she worked for many years. "They never let me say 'I can't,' or 'I shouldn't.' They never let me think I couldn't do something.

"And my mom's been a great encouragement, even though she's far away and struggling with her own illness," Linda continues. "I just have to call her to hear: 'You can get through this. You can do it, Linda. You can do it if you try!'"

After experiencing devastating burns in a plane crash, Merrill Womach shares this:

> *Doctors and nurses have needles and pills to help you get through physical suffering. But what about the pain inside that comes from loneliness or fear? . . . Only God can help you bear that kind of pain. You are not alone. He is with you! When you feel lonely call out to Him. He will hear you and help you. When you are afraid, reach out and He will take your hand.*

MERRILL WOMACH, *TESTED BY FIRE*

The Lord will guide you continually,
and satisfy your needs in parched places,
and make your bones strong;
and you shall be like a watered garden,
like a spring of water,
whose waters never fail.

Isaiah 58:11 NRSV

DANCE

Your soul can dance though pain is here.
Call healing music to your ear.
Spot emotion's fickle turning,
Leap in love,
Stretch hopes,
Master fear's deep strains.
Dare to dance both health and pain.
However clumsy, long, or fleeting,
We dance life well if grace is leading.

. . . God is totally sovereign in sickness and totally sovereign in healing. Sometimes He directly sends sickness, other times He lets it come naturally. Sometimes He intervenes in the sickness and heals, other times He lets the patient die. Occasionally He gives explanations for His behavior; usually, however, He lets us wonder. He is God.

PEG RANKIN, *YET WILL I TRUST HIM*

REFILLING THE EMPTINESS

Illness has come like a thief in the night and stolen the innocence of daily, take-it-for-granted life. In God's hands, it can become an opportunity for renewal and discovering what—and who—really matters.

You have turned my mourning into dancing . . . and clothed me with joy.

Psalm 30:11 NRSV

HAPPENSTANCE

Help me recover from this ambush of illness, Great Physician, and the worry it brings. Reassure my fearful heart that my sickness was never intended, it just happened. Bodies break down, parts age, and minds weary. Your assurance gives me strength to hang on.

... listening is one of the first, best steps in helping your friend to win the emotional, mental and spiritual battles that accompany illness. A listening friend faces your inner struggles with you, bearing the burden at your side, leaving you more energy to fight the battle for life.

ELIZABETH DEAN BURNHAM, *WHEN YOUR FRIEND IS DYING*

OCTOBER 1979

Why does everyone cry?
Why do I?
Why does Mommy let walls come between us?
Why do those who treat me hurt me?
Why, in an ambulance, did Daddy hold me
  tight?
Why when the doctor said "Remission," did
  everybody jump and cry?
Should I?

> "*W*ho touched me?" Jesus
> asked.... "Someone touched me; I know
> that power has gone out from me."
>
> Then the woman, seeing that she could not go
> unnoticed, came trembling and fell at his feet.
> In the presence of all the people, she told why
> she had touched him and how she had been
> instantly healed. Then he said to her,
> "Daughter, your faith has healed you.
> Go in peace."
>
> *Luke 8:45–48 NIV*

IT'S ALL IN THE FAMILY

Our families suffer, too, O God, as illness runs
its course. Faces show strain from trying not to
worry; voices sound too bright from unshed
tears. Strengthen them for the grueling task that
awaits; their support is life-sustaining.

> *W*ait on the Lord: be of good courage,
> and he shall strengthen thine heart.
>
> *P*salm 27:14 KJV

Once I slept in a hospital in a concentration camp. Many people were ill and many died. In the night, I heard people calling and I went to them. I was ill myself, but not so seriously that I couldn't do this—I went to everyone who called.

... It was in that concentration camp hospital that I experienced God's use of sick people to help others around them.

CORRIE TEN BOOM, *HE CARES, HE COMFORTS*

MOODY BLUES

Illness makes our moods like a children's wind-up toy, crazily up one minute, flat down the next; we cry and laugh, we worry and celebrate!

Getting well is hard, complicated work. May God lead us into full recovery, but carefully— we're still a bit unpredictable.

STAY NEARBY

Are you here, Lord? I've never felt lonelier than in this illness. Sometimes I feel easier saying a child's prayer or repeating a familiar verse— anything to connect with you. Hear me, O God, for I feel like a stranger.

I'm comforted, for just the simple act of praying reminds me you are in the middle of not only the illness, but also the getting well. You are where you're needed, my steadfast companion.

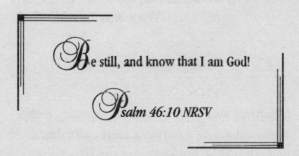

Be still, and know that I am God!

Psalm 46:10 NRSV

And what if healing does not come to us?
Even then we do not need to lose heart nor
faith. We will believe that God's grace is
sufficient, that his power is made perfect in
weakness. We shall look up, lift up our heads,
and look for the coming King. With his coming
will come also complete wholeness and
vibrant health.

MILDRED TENGBOM, *WHY WASTE YOUR ILLNESS?*

O Joy that seekest me through pain,
I cannot close my heart to thee;
I trace the rainbow thro' the rain,
And feel the promise is not vain
That morn shall tearless be.

GEORGE MATHESON, "O LOVE THAT
WILT NOT LET ME GO"

. . . when I was ill in a hospital for many weeks
some years ago, I felt very lonely, perplexed,
and miserable. But suffering can be what

businessmen call a "frozen asset." . . . while
suffering continues we may be unable to see
anything remotely like an asset about it; but
gradually, . . . we can take such an attitude to it
that we can do what Jesus did: offer it to God
and in so doing help him turn it into a victory.

LESLIE B. WEATHERHEAD, *SALUTE TO A*
SUFFERER

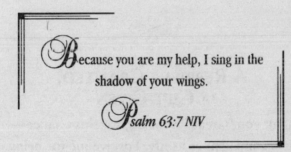

*B*ecause you are my help, I sing in the
shadow of your wings.

*P*salm 63:7 NIV

SHEEP OF GOD'S PASTURE

Despite today's valley of shadow and sickness, I
know you, shepherd of my soul, will continue
restoring me as I move through treatment to the
safe meadow of wellness.

WAITING WITH ROOM
FOR ONE MORE

Sitting here in this waiting room, O God, time drags and fears festers. Remake worry into energized, active prayers, into trust in the process of healing and recovery. We're scooting over to make room for you, a companion for the waiting.

A REPRIEVE GRANTED,
A GIFT GIVEN

Thank you, Great Physician, for this chance— this second chance at life. Forgive me for being surprised, as if healing were beyond possibility and your intention.

Chapter 3:

WHEN THE DARKNESS WON'T LIFT

Depression: It's a word we use casually, lightly ignoring the fact that true depression—whether its cause is biological or brought about by life events—can be utterly devastating. The depressed person is emotionally paralyzed, cut off from the stream of daily life. And the condition is self-perpetuating: Just finding the energy to seek help can seem like an insurmountable task.

So how do people find their way out of the darkness and into the light? The motivations to seek help and the ways people find to lift themselves out of the pit of depression are as varied as individual personalities. And God is always there, quietly encouraging us to seek the light.

*I would rather walk with God in the dark
than go alone in the light.*

MARY GARDINER BRAINARD

A BURDEN SHARED

Gerry had not always felt depressed. In his earlier years, any inkling of sadness had been quickly washed away with a quick nip of the bottle—or days of binge drinking. He had been sober for years now, though, and was proud of it. Yet it was hard to know what to do when his old demon of depression came to call. He did not always immediately catch on to what was happening; sometimes, what he thought was a moment of sadness that would be normal for anyone turned into months of lingering malaise and the feeling that life wasn't even worth living.

At the age of 74, Gerry had hoped to be done with depression. True, it came less frequently than in earlier years, but when the sadness set in, it was hard even to get out of bed in the morning. Since he no longer worked, Gerry had to make an effort to stay active and in touch with others who might help him see the world in a positive light.

Gerry's new minister came to call on a day when the darkness was settling in around him.

"You seem a bit down," Reverend Morton commented. "Anything wrong?"

Gerry took a risk and poured out his difficult history, ending with, "And I guess depression is just something I have to live with."

"Depression has many causes and takes many forms," the pastor said. "But it's not something you have to face alone. Why not get your church involved? Let them pray you through this."

"Oh, no," Gerry protested. "I don't want anyone to know about my problem."

"You'd be surprised how many others in the congregation struggle with depression, too," Morton replied. "Maybe we could start a depression support group."

And so, reluctantly, Gerry let himself be talked into joining the group. Reverend Morton started the first meeting out, but it wasn't long before a group of individuals who had thought they must battle depression alone found themselves looking forward to the Thursday meetings. Even on those days when they really wanted to stay home rather than face the world, support group members dragged themselves to the place that offered understanding, friendship, sanctuary.

On the six days they were not together, the group had a standing prayer time when each member prayed for the others. "Lift his spirits, Lord." "God, give her hope." "Help him feel loved." The prayers were simple and let even the most depressed know every day that others cared for them.

And Gerry? His depression still comes and goes, as it always has. But he never has to face it alone anymore.

Our experiences resemble a jigsaw puzzle. . . . When it is all ready, we shall find that the dark pieces of the puzzle were as important in the

*completion of the full beauty of the pattern as
the bright sections. The dark background will
only bring out in bolder and more gorgeous
relief the figures in the picture, in the center of
which will be His lovely face . . .*

M. R. DeHaan, M.D., *Broken Things*

It is you who light my lamp;
the Lord, my God, lights up my darkness.
This God—his way is perfect;
the promise of the Lord proves true;
he is a shield for all who take refuge in him.

Psalm 18:28, 30 NRSV

A Crushing Pain

Of the many ways to suffer, I feel all of them in
this firestorm of sadness. It robs my sleep, saps
my strength, and changes me so much I hardly
recognize myself. Ease my misery, Lord. Clear
my mind as though washing streaks from a window. Hold me when I cry, releasing feelings that

keep me sick; send others to hold me, too. Remind me that this pain is temporary and can be relieved, just like my worries.

My soul melts away for sorrow; strengthen me according to your word.

Psalm 119:28 NRSV

. . . there is a depression among true Christians, with the individuals who are out of the center of God's directive will. The most unhappy person in the world is a child of God out of the Father's control. The cure is to return!

F. L. WHITESELL, *THE CURE FOR DEPRESSION*

Do you get anxious at sunrise because all you can see is the tiny rim of the sun? No, because you know that if you wait long enough you will see the sun in all its brilliance. The same

is true of God's plan for your life. You will never see everything in advance; but if you wait long enough, God always reveals His will.

So relax! God is in charge. Soon enough the darkness will vanish, and all that is vague will be made perfectly clear.

RAY PRITCHARD, *THE ROAD BEST TRAVELED— KNOWING GOD'S WILL FOR YOUR LIFE*

LIVING IN THE LIGHT

Katie remembers standing in a field behind her house, trying to cry. Her sadness didn't come from anything specific; she knew she needed to cry but no tears would come. "I think I was depressed, even as a child," Katie recounts. "It wasn't until I developed anorexia that I had to face the sadness that clouded over me. When I confided my problem to a close friend, she urged me to get help and, with my mother's encouragement, I joined an eating disorders support group."

Eventually, Katie met her husband and moved across the country, but when the excitement of her new life died down, the depression returned along with anorexia symptoms. "I just wanted to stay in bed all day." A doctor put her on tranquilizers but they did not provide the help she needed. It wasn't until Katie was tested at a neuropsychiatric institute that her severe depression was diagnosed.

Thy word is a lamp unto my feet, and a light unto my path.

Psalm 119:105 KJV

A treatment was prescribed: antidepressants and counseling. And it worked. In the 15 years since Katie went on medication, she has twice tried to go off it but has quickly discovered that, in her case, the medicine is what enables her to lead a healthy and happy life. Anyone meeting her today would be surprised to learn of her past anorexia and depression.

"With me, depression is biological," Katie explains. "Without antidepressants, I would once again be overwhelmed by sleeplessness, lethargy, and a general overwhelming sadness. I always know that the depression could rear its ugly head if I don't take care of myself."

In Katie's case, strong support from family and friends helped guide her toward a medical solution to her problem. "And I always attended church services even through the difficult times, though I didn't exactly know why. Now that I have children, I'm active in a church community, and that adds to my life, too."

Having lived through the darkness, Katie is grateful for a life lived in the light that good mental health brings to her and her family.

The One whose love and wisdom we question is at our side, reading our thoughts and knowing us as no other. He silently pursues the beneficial end of the trial and sorrow He permits.... Our heavenly Father, who corrects us because He loves us, is too wise to err in

His government of our lives, and too good to err through malice. Therefore, we can safely trust ourselves to His care...

HERBERT LOCKYER,
DARK THREADS THE WEAVER NEEDS

*F*eed the hungry! Help those in trouble! Then your light will shine out from the darkness, and the darkness around you shall be as bright as day.

*I*saiah 58:10 TLB

Let me meditate upon the dark nights through which I have come, the sinister things from which I have been delivered—and have a grateful heart.

**PETER MARSHALL, *THE PRAYERS
OF PETER MARSHALL***

It is down
makes
up seem
taller
black
sharpens white...

After silence
each sound
sings
dull clay
shines the
bright coin
in the pot
lemon
honeys its
sweet sequel
and my dark
distress
shows comfort
to be doubly
heaven-sent

Luci Shaw, "Of Consolation"

NIGHT-LIGHTS

Reach out to me, a child again, lost, frightened, and alone with few answers for comfort. Stay with me until I fall asleep and be here if I awake scared. Let me be a child tonight, Lord. Tomorrow I'll be big and strong and all grown-up, but for now, find me, hold me.

"Nay, none of these!"
Speak, soul, aright in His holy sight
Whose eye looks still
And steadily on thee through the night:
"To do His will!"

JOHN GREENLEAF WHITTIER, "MY SOUL AND I"

I will turn the darkness into light before them and make the rough places smooth.

Isaiah 42:16 NIV

I was often filled with despair.

*What kept me afloat, what kept me going, were
the times I shared alone with God. Times
when he gave me hope and a reason to live.*

*The situation did not really change much. But
in those times, when I let him, God always
lifted me up...*

PETER LORD, *HEARING GOD*

*Great faith is not the faith that walks always in
the light and knows no darkness, but the faith
that perseveres in spite of God's seeming silences,
and that faith will most certainly and surely get
its reward.*

FATHER ANDREW SDC

PRIORITIES

As a college senior, Andrea was highly
recruited for employment. "Having so
many job offers when I was barely 21 years old
was wonderfully overwhelming," she remem-

bers. "It made all the work I had put into getting good grades worth the effort." She chose a public relations firm in a large eastern city and moved there after graduation.

"In the beginning, I didn't see how seductive the work was," she says, a slight frown on her face. "I could hardly believe that I was going to work each day in a high-rise building with such talented coworkers. I didn't realize the pressure I was under or how desperately I wanted to succeed."

Success, Andrea figured, would come if she worked hard enough. So she came in early and left late and spent most of her weekends at home focused on projects that would look good in her portfolio.

"In the beginning, I at least made it to worship on Sundays but soon, even that got left out of my busy schedule. The bible study I'd been committed to in college, regular exercise, eating healthy—there didn't seem to be time to worry about all of that. I was determined to prove myself, to show that even though I was young, I could make it playing with the big kids."

For all her hard work, Andrea did not receive the pats on the back she had anticipated. Her progress in college had been determined by grades; her current supervisor didn't give her much feedback on how well she was doing. She put in even more hours trying to prove her worth.

> *M*y God turns my darkness into light.
>
> *Psalm 18:28 NIV*

Then, one Monday morning, Andrea could not get out of bed. "I lay there, panic gripping at my chest, unable to move. It was time to get up and go to work but I couldn't even throw back the covers." It was the first sign of depression. Some days she called in sick, other times she went to work but the days passed in a fog. "I was tired all the time, living in shades of gray rather than colors. I couldn't seem to muster enthusiasm for work. I spent hours at home just sitting in a chair looking out the window."

Andrea's depression deepened, though she had yet to give a name to the condition. "I couldn't even feel," she says. "My job productivity dropped off but no one at work seemed to notice. Then I felt really inadequate and unneeded."

Beth, a college friend, came to town one day. "You look awful!" she worried. "What's going on?" Beth was astute enough to recognize depression and stayed an extra week to care for her worn-down friend. She not only insisted that Andrea take a week off work to catch up on sleep, she stocked the kitchen with healthy foods and helped Andrea sign up at a nearby fitness club. And, even though Beth was Jewish, she took Andrea to a local church worship service. "I know this used to mean a lot to you," she said. "You need church friends to help balance your life."

Since the depression had been caused by exhaustion, lack of exercise and nutritious food, and the self-imposed pressures the young woman had placed on herself, Beth's remedies helped the darkness lift quickly. Now Andrea still works in public relations but she has learned that her job is only one part of her life.

She joined the church choir and volleyball team and got a poodle from the animal shelter.

"Depression was a scary time for me. Life hardly seemed worth living," Andrea says. "I learned that I need friends and I need to take care of myself if I am going to be healthy. Once Beth helped me know I needed help, I found there were lots of people ready to share their lives with me. I went through a really dark time but now I'm okay."

COLLECTING SOUVENIRS OF HOPE

I need to believe beyond the present darkness, for it threatens to stop me in my tracks. Steady me, God of infinite resources, as I collect my beliefs like candles to light and move through this dark tunnel of doubt and uncertainty. Inspire me to add new truths as they reveal themselves in my life. Along the way, help my unbelief.

> *B*y day the Lord commands his steadfast
> love, and at night his song is with me.
>
> *P*salm 42:8 NRSV

*No one is exempt from tragedy or
disappointment—God himself was not exempt.
Jesus offered no immunity, no way out of the
unfairness, but rather a way through it to the
other side. Just as Good Friday demolished
the instinctive belief that this life is supposed
to be fair, Easter Sunday followed with its
startling clue to the riddle of the universe. Out
of the darkness, a bright light shone.*

PHILIP YANCEY, *DISAPPOINTMENT WITH GOD*

REACHING OUT IN COURAGE

It takes great courage to heal, Lord, great
energy to reach out from this darkness to touch
the hem of your garment and ask for healing.

Bless the brave voices telling nightmare tales of dreadful wounds to the gifted healers of this world. Together, sufferers and healers are binding up damaged parts and laying down burdens carried so long.

Though like the wanderer,
  The sun gone down,
Darkness be over me,
  My rest a stone;
Yet in my dreams I'd be
Nearer, my God, to Thee,
  Nearer to Thee!
. . . Then, with my waking thoughts
  Bright with Thy praise,
Out of my stony griefs,
  Bethel I'll raise;
So by my woes to be
Nearer my God, to Thee,
  Nearer to Thee!

SARAH FLOWER ADAMS, "NEARER TO THEE"

ANYTHING IS POSSIBLE:
A PRAYER FOR BLOOMING

There is every reason to give up and give in, steadfast God, for days are a struggling drudgery. When I falter, remind me that with you I am as resilient as crocuses blooming in the snow.

Why are you downcast, O my soul?
Why so disturbed within me?
Put your hope in God,
for I will yet praise him,
my Savior and my God.

Psalm 42:11 NIV

Nowhere in God's Book are we instructed to live morbidly and sadly. God does not intend that his children should go on being sad and unhappy. The apostle Paul, even in the midst of severe trial, instructs us, "rejoice and again I say rejoice." In another place he writes,

"...I have learned, in whatsoever state I am,
therein to be content." I'm thankful that he
included the word learned.

GLADYS KOOIMAN,
WHEN DEATH TAKES A FATHER

CAVE WALKERS

We wander like children lost in a cave,
perilously close to the edge of despair. Unable to
see where we're going, we crouch in fear rather
than risk falling while searching for an exit.
Nudge us beyond fear; send us guides who have
traveled dark passages before.

Sometimes when reading accounts of innocent
prisoners facing death, I become impressed
with the intensity of life that they seem to be
experiencing. The importance of every
moment is heightened as death awaits its
prey.... In a strange way I feel left out...it's
not that I covet their pain.... But I do become

*aware that I am reading stories of individuals
who are experiencing a fullness of life that
very few people know.*

PEG RANKIN, *YET WILL I TRUST HIM*

*H*e has sent me to bind up the
brokenhearted,
to proclaim freedom for the captives
and release from darkness for the prisoners,
to proclaim the year of the Lord's favor
and the day of vengeance of our God,
to comfort all who mourn,
and provide for those who grieve in Zion—
to bestow on them a crown of beauty
instead of ashes,
the oil of gladness
instead of mourning,
and a garment of praise
instead of a spirit of despair.

*I*saiah 61:1–3a NIV

NEVER TO BE ALONE

I cannot wander so far in any direction, vigilant God, that you are not already there.

Love is too often like a glow-worm, showing but little light except it be in the midst of surrounding darkness. Hope itself is like a star—not to be seen in the sunshine of prosperity, and only to be discovered in the night of adversity.

CHARLES HADDON SPURGEON,
MORNING BY MORNING

Hope springs eternal in the human breast:
Man never is, but always to be, blest.
The soul, uneasy and confin'd from home
Rests and expatiates in a life to come.

ALEXANDER POPE, "AN ESSAY ON MAN"

LIGHT IN DARKNESS

No darkness is black enough to hide you, Lord, for there is always light even if I sometimes misplace it. Just when I'm ready to give up, there it shines through caregivers, family, friends; through my renewed energy to choose treatments and recovery. I'm absolutely certain you are the sender of this light.

So praise God for the dark days when often our sweetest lessons are learned...

VANCE HAVNER, *ALL THE DAYS*

Finally beloved, whatever is true, whatever is honorable, whatever is just, whatever is pure, whatever is pleasing, whatever is commendable, if there is any excellence and if there is anything worthy of praise, think about these things.

Philippians 4:8 NRSV

FAMILY AND FRIENDS, DOWN-HEARTED WATCHERS

In the face of the seemingly impenetrable darkness where our special one suffers, I feel unequal to the task of going to visit. Let my reluctant, bumbling visits be a bridge from the depths of bleak illness back into a waiting world.

Now God be prais'd that to believing souls
Gives light in darkness, comfort in despair!

WILLIAM SHAKESPEARE, *KING HENRY VI*

It was weeks and months that Tom wrestled, in his own soul, in darkness and sorrow...

When a heavy weight presses the soul to the lowest level at which endurance is possible, there is an instant and desperate effort of every physical and moral nerve to throw off the weight; and hence the heaviest anguish

*often precedes a return tide of joy and
courage.*

So it was now with Tom.

HARRIET BEECHER STOWE,
UNCLE TOM'S CABIN,
IN THE CHAPTER TITLED "THE VICTORY"

SIGNS OF POSSIBILITY

From my dark corner I look up and see wings
fluttering against the window and know that a
God who can make a butterfly from a cater-
pillar can surely make something new of me.

*Hope is a lover's staff; walk hence with that,
And manage it against despairing thoughts.*

WILLIAM SHAKESPEARE,
THE TWO GENTLEMEN OF VERONA

...for all of us there are going to be some tears and sighs, some sorrow and sadness, some dark periods of disappointment and despair....

Will I accept them calmly as coming from the hand of my Heavenly Father for my own well-being?

W. PHILLIP KELLER, *AS A TREE GROWS*

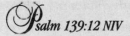

Even the darkness will not be dark to
you;
the night will shine like the day,
for darkness is as light to you.

Psalm 139:12 NIV

COUNTING ON IT

Even now, I know God gives me strength to match my weaknesses.

Chapter 4:

WHEN THERE'S TENSION AT HOME

Many of us think of home as our refuge from life's stresses, our "port in a storm." Within our own four walls we expect to find acceptance, unconditional love, encouragement when times are rough, and reassurance that we are worthy people. And we have a right to expect these things, just as our family members have a right to expect them from us.

But we're only human. Sometimes tensions interfere with the loving atmosphere of the family, preventing us from receiving and giving the warmth we crave. Stresses can come from inside or outside the home, and they can be devastating. We have to resist the urge to pull away from each other in anger. And when the wounds received are too deep, healing may take a lifetime. Solutions can be painful at first, but with God's help, they can be found.

WINNERS AND LOSERS: FLIPPING A COIN

On one hand, the job offer was a great opportunity for Steve's career; on the other, it was a potential disaster because it would uproot his family. Ellen had put her career on hold to stay home with the couple's three children. She'd invested herself in schools, medical and caregiving networks, a babysitting co-op, and most importantly, her parents who lived nearby. They were enjoying the grand-children and coming to rely on Ellen's support as they faced retirement.

"Now's not the time to move," Ellen insisted.

"Oh, yes it is," Steve challenged.

One had to lose for the other to win. Each inter-preted the other's position as proof of disloyalty. Either way, it was an invitation to the next step of their life, which they were ready to take sepa-rately after Steve accused Ellen of being tied to her parents, more daughter than wife.

Sacrificial or selfish: Surely there was a spot in between. With help from a counselor, they learned to say "I need" instead of "I must have." Ellen needed Steve, Steve needed Ellen—the God who had joined them could surely help. Looking back, they saw how many times this had already happened. Compromise began to look less like losing. Both of them choosing to move toward the center—toward the relationship—rather than defending separate positions.

The rain came down, the streams rose, and the winds blew and beat against that house; yet it did not fall, because it had its foundation on the rock.

Matthew 7:25 NIV

Steve decided to pause on his move up the career ladder, promising Ellen time to renegotiate her relationship with her parents. She got a part-time job and began weaning her folks from premature dependence on her.

By the time of Steve's next promotion and relocation opportunity, Ellen was able to grieve and go on, taking her considerable skills as mother, neighbor, and friend into a new community. Steve, no longer seeing Ellen's reluctance to move as rejection of him, arranged his schedule so he could tend the children while Ellen worked at night, moving up her own career ladder so that together they could have the life they both wanted.

And the grandparents?

They learned to travel, to volunteer. Ellen hooked them up to e-mail, a surprisingly successful idea born, Ellen says, of desperation to bring her parents into the world where she was choosing to go.

"That's the key," she and Steve agree, "choosing. We chose our relationship as top priority. That makes it simpler to quit thinking like winners and losers. There's no future in that."

We are often hindered from giving up our treasures to the Lord out of fear for their safety; this is especially true when those treasures are loved relatives and friends. But we need have no such fears. Our Lord came not to destroy but to save. Everything is safe which we commit to Him, and nothing is really safe which is not so committed.

A. W. TOZER, *THE PURSUIT OF GOD*

WITH THE HEART OF A CHILD

There are broken places in our family, and it's hard, serious work patching them up. In the midst of all there is to do, we feel God leading us outdoors to splash in spring rains, across beaches, and into snowdrifts where we are rejuvenated by the sheer pleasure of playing. Laughter, in God's splendid creation, is good for heart, mind, body, soul, and most certainly our struggling family.

*Oh, God, dear God, God who created him in
the first place, please help my blind, naive,
misguided child...
He's trying to find himself through sheer
physical sensation. He's trying drugs to
"expand his mind."
And I am sick with fear. My flesh goes rotten
at the thought, my blood is water in my
veins...
Help me, help me, please.
But first—help him.*

MARJORIE HOLMES, *WHO AM I, GOD?*

*Thank you,
my little ones, for bringing with you
tender hearts and innocent eyes.
I love the way
you sprinkle your contagious giggles
all over my life.*

ROBIN JONES GUNN, *MOTHERING BY HEART*

He has sent me to comfort the brokenhearted.

Isaiah 61:1 TLB

*What wears me out
are little things:
angels minus
shining wings.
Forgive me, Lord,
if I have whined;
... it takes so much
to keep them shined;
yet each small rub
has its reward,
for they have blessed me.*

*Thank You,
Lord.*

RUTH BELL GRAHAM,
SITTING BY MY LAUGHING FIRE...

MENDING A BROKEN
WEDDING RING

We teeter on the edge of splitting up, Lord; help us use this interval as a wake-up call. You link our two halves and can re-create us whole.

If faith wins the battles within, love wins them without.

NORMAN GRUBB, *THE SPONTANEOUS YOU*

BRIDGING THE
DAMAGED DISTANCE

Sally was angry at Jeff's choice not to travel home for Christmas. Jeff resisted Sally's need for him to do so.

Brother and sister, both had good reasons for their actions: Like too many people, each had been abused by a relative. Therapy and time had begun their healing, but it was early days yet. The scabs over the wounds were so new both Sally and Jeff feared a reunion might knock them off. And yet they longed to be together, something that hadn't happened since they had left the abusive family.

Perhaps distance is best, Sally decided, trying to put on a bright face as she hung a holiday wreath on her front door. Perhaps not, Jeff reconsidered, making secret flight reservations.

Christmas Eve lunch was ready at Sally's, the guests already seated. A knock on her door, and suddenly there was Jeff: brother, comrade, friend.

Who would presume to explain what urged Jeff to venture, Sally to insist, except that love is a map between people in all sorts of relationships? At its intersection of faithful hope, family members become companions in healing from even the most awful wounds.

Peace unto this house, I pray,
Keep terror and despair away;
Shield it from evil and let sin
Never find lodging room within.
May never in these walls be heard
The hateful or accusing word....

Lord, this humble house we'd keep
Sweet with play and calm with sleep.
Help us so that we may give
Beauty to the lives we live.
Let Thy love and let Thy grace
Shine upon our dwelling place.

EDGAR GUEST, "PRAYER FOR THE HOME"

OPERATION WISDOM

Kids do the dumbest things, skirting disaster.
And while it's not possible to put an old head
on young shoulders, O God, I would if I could.
Help me find ways that won't alienate and yet
will protect my impetuous young ones.

NOBODY'S LISTENING

Guide my quarrelsome, divided family to common ground, God of reconciliation; mediate our negotiations; inspire solutions.

I will study the way that is blameless. When shall I attain it? I will walk with integrity of heart within my house.

Psalm 101:2 LB

Children have a keen sense of being forsaken and abandoned when they are deprived of one or both parents. Do we lead them to the God who understands, fills the void, and supplies their needs? Have we given them the assurance that there is one Friend who will never, never leave them nor forsake them?

EVELYN CHRISTENSON, *GAINING THROUGH LOSING*

It is important to cultivate a genuine mood of hope in your home. Hope is not a "cross-your-fingers" kind of dreamy-eyed sentiment. Hope is the solid conviction that God has a genuine, custom-made, blessed plan for you and your family, and that He is totally committed to seeing it fulfilled!

JACK HAYFORD, *GLORY ON YOUR HOUSE*

Let us then, remember these three jewel words: love, cherish, and honor. They may pave the royal road to the utmost in domestic happiness for all of us.

TOM WESTWOOD, *THE CHRISTIAN HOUSEHOLD*

*W*e who are strong ought to put up with the failings of the weak, and not to please ourselves.

*R*omans 15:1 NRSV

Rising From the Ruins of a Marriage

I never meant to be a failure, Lord, never meant to break commitments. But I am and I did. Comfort me, for I mourn the loss of innocence that crumbled beneath the knowledge that I couldn't stay in the marriage and be okay. Forgive my failures; heal my regrets and fortify my courage. Help me grieve and go on free from toxic, wasteful hate. And as I do, help me forgive those left behind.

If we are wise, we will ask God to help us help each other bloom.

Betty Malz, *Women in Tune*

It is impossible for me to overstate the need for prayer in the fabric of family life. Not simply as a shield against danger. . . . Being able to bow in prayer as the day begins or

ends gives expression to the frustrations and
concerns that might not otherwise be ventilated.
On the other end of that prayer line is a loving
heavenly Father who has promised to hear
and answer our petitions.

DR. JAMES DOBSON, *LOVE FOR A LIFETIME*

BATTLE OF WILLS

Help us, loving Parent, treat our frustrating
children with the same strengthening patience
and trust you extend to us.

A SNACK THOUGHT
PINK-KA-PINKKK!
Like a pot full of popcorn
The voice of a mob
Begins with one exploding kernel.
Like an unruly mob
Families sometimes sizzle and explode
Unable to turn down the heat,
Unwilling to avoid either kettle or fire.

It's only a snack thought,
But
If truth shakes down
Guarded by the lid of kindness,
Families can survive heat,
Escape hardness,
And learn to nourish.

Open-Handed Sharing

When feelings are hurt, Wise Physician, we curl in on ourselves like orange rinds, withholding even the possibility of reconciliation. Help us open up to new possibilities for righting wrong and sharing love without reservation, as the orange blossom offers its fragrance, the fruit its zesty sweetness.

When people know that we will not hurt them, they cease being defensive. In the presence of gentleness, family members are more prone to really listen to what we're saying.

Disagreements are less likely to become emotional issues in which saving face takes prominence. Power struggles are diminished and reasonable discussion can occur because respect and sensitivity is shown for one another.

WAYNE A. MACK, *YOUR FAMILY, GOD'S WAY*

May God who gives patience, steadiness, and encouragement help you to live in complete harmony with each other—each with the attitude of Christ toward the other.

Romans 15:5 TLB

Don't become overly discouraged if you have problems with your children. God understands. He has problems with His kids, too.

GIGI GRAHAM TCHIVIDJIAN, *WEATHER OF THE HEART*

. . . a parent's love is not enough. A child's life continues to need the miracle touch of God.

RON HUTCHCRAFT, 5 *NEEDS YOUR CHILD MUST HAVE MET AT HOME*

HOME RUN

Kathy was the last to suspect: Rick was having an affair. When he took the children ice skating on Kathy's school nights, Rick also brought Valerie, a newly widowed family friend, and her youngsters. At first Kathy praised Rick for his support of a friend in need. It wasn't until one of the children mentioned an outing she had been unaware of that Kathy became uneasy. Confronted, Rick reminded Kathy it had been her idea to go back to school instead of staying home with her family, "the way Valerie does."

Stung, Kathy began to be supermom, superwife. Eventually, though, Rick wound up sleeping in the den and working late . . . if, indeed, that was where he was. Valerie stopped calling Kathy to "chat," as had been their pattern; Kathy withdrew her daughter from Valerie's scout troop and quizzed the children about Rick's activities until he accused Kathy of having the children spy on him. Fighting, even in whispers, is hard to hide: Family life was an armed truce, with the children caught in the crossfire. Until 8-year-old Jessica ran away.

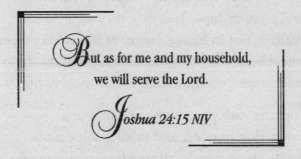

But as for me and my household, we will serve the Lord.

Joshua 24:15 NIV

Rick found her sitting in the bleachers at the soccer field. "You and Mama hurt my ears," the child sobbed. "I hate home."

"We'll fix it," her father promised, shaken to see how close he had come to losing his family. He had gambled with the roots of it, and only God knew whether it could be salvaged. He vowed to try as he drove home, his daughter tearfully hiccuping beside him.

He and Kathy conferred briefly, then called a family meeting. They all joined hands and prayed for quieter voices and forgiveness. They promised the children, and one another, that they would come up with ways to build a new—not just patch the old—family.

Finding supportive, informative help was step one for Rick and Kathy; step two was healing old relationships. Together, they went to see Valerie, not to blame, but to explain. Like them, she'd been caught in the lie that cheating could substitute for negotiating rough spots in life.

Talking with one another, talking to a counselor, praying, and talking some more healed the wounds, although scars remained, for trouble is part of life just as night is part of creation. The family took up sailing and camping, where God's renewing presence reminded them that just as spring follows winter, a new season of family was upon them. Winter, they say now, 30 years later, was just a little longer that year.

Love is patient, love is kind. It does not envy, it does not boast, it is not proud. It is not rude, it is not self-seeking, it is not easily angered, it keeps no record of wrongs. Love does not delight in evil but rejoices with the truth. It always protects, always trusts, always hopes, always perseveres. Love never fails.

1 Corinthians 13:4–8 NIV

Little by little, I grew more patient with Darcy. God was showing himself faithful. He did love me after all, and he cared about our family. I was thrilled and over time grew more confident that God did have a plan for me to be a loving mother. In time, he even healed the relationship between Larry and me. . . . Eventually I knew that God had indeed delivered me from being an abusive mother.

KATHY COLLARD MILLER, *COUNTING TO 10 ISN'T ENOUGH*

TEENS TAKING US ALL THROUGH TURMOIL

As fickle as the weather, teens change moods, clothes, and values, disrupting the family unfortunate enough to be in the way. In the struggle to grow up and away, they go too far, and we are left in the wake like a torn tail on a kite. God's is the shoulder to lean on while we catch our breath.

. . . even though we may fail as parents, there is a God who loves our children more than we do and He never fails. No matter how many mistakes we as parents make, there is still hope that a wayward child will respond to the power of the Holy Spirit, make a decision for Christ, and come back to a life pleasing to God . . . never lose hope, never give up, never stop praying.

STEPHEN ARTERBURN AND JIM BURNS,
WHEN LOVE IS NOT ENOUGH

*We have to be willing to forgive, because
mistakes are going to be made. There is going
to be anger and even, at times, deliberate
hurtful words, so understanding and flexibility
are required. And it is crucial during times of
crisis to maintain an overriding sense of
permanence. For Rosalynn and me, the
marriage vows have been a powerful
stabilizing force. Largely because we consider
these pledges inviolable, we have survived our
differences now for fifty years.*

JIMMY CARTER, *LIVING FAITH*

DECIDING FACTOR

The marriage is not working; should I go or
stay? Unrealized dreams litter my path and the
future—alone—looks better than the past—
together. Is this temporary boredom or perma-
nent trouble? Facing this reality is the first step
in healing; your grace is promise enough to
keep going until I know.

If I am right, Thy grace impart,
  Still in the right to stay;
If I am wrong, oh teach my heart
  To find that better way.

ALEXANDER POPE, "AN ESSAY ON MAN"

*B*e angry but do not sin; do not let
the sun go down on your anger.

*E*phesians 4:26 NRSV

WAITING

Waiting for a chill to pass before rising at
  dawn
For water to boil for tea
For the mail to come
For children to barge from the gate through
  the door
For their father to return from a journey
For darkness to force the family inside
For others to take turns at a game
For fire embers to die

For glances of love to forgive the pettiness of
  my day
For sleep to come.
Lord, remind me to wait when my temper
  flares;
  To wait past hurt or hate for words that heal.
. . . when I was a child, I needed love most
when I deserved it the least.

JOHN MAXWELL, *BREAKTHROUGH PARENTING*

CERTAINLY NOT MY CHOICE

This is not a choice I would make, for me or for
the one who went against my standards, my
hopes. It's a riddle, O God, why you give us
freedom to choose. It can break our hearts.
Comfort me as I cope with a choice not mine;
forgive any role I had in it. Help me separate
doer from deed as I pass on your words to all
". . . nothing can separate us." Not even poor
choices I sometimes make myself.

*Train a child in the way he should go,
and when he is old he will not turn from it.*

Proverbs 22:6 NIV

*There is no doubt in my mind that my sister
  loves me.
But there is probably doubt in hers that I love
  her...
I really do love her, Lord, but maybe I don't
know how to love as you want me to love her.
Please forgive me.
I want to be my sister's forever friend...
Teach me to love my sister, Lord. Help us both
learn more about real friendship from facing
together the problems that come up today.*

CLAIR G. COSBY, *LORD, HELP ME
LOVE MY SISTER*

*Home isn't a place. It's knowing we belong.
It's where the sharp angles and rough edges*

*of our individual selves somehow manage to
fit in with the angles and edges of others to
form a whole.*

PHYLLIS HOBE, *WHEN LOVE ISN'T EASY*

GOING THE DISTANCE
FROM A DISTANCE

There comes a time when children must take
what belongs to them—not just stuff stored in
the garage, but consequences of choices they are
now making. Parents can go only so far, then
must watch from a loving, caring distance, even
through tears of disappointment and worry.

A SEASON OF RENEWAL

Hearts frozen by betrayal can be thawed by the
touch of the God of Easter who brings to life
what at first looks hopeless.

*D*on't worry about anything; instead, pray about everything; tell God your needs and don't forget to thank him for the answers. If you do this you will experience God's peace, which is far more wonderful than the human mind can understand. His peace will keep your thoughts and your hearts quiet and at rest as you trust in Christ Jesus.

*P*hilippians 4:6–7 TLB

We need to leave the past with God. In faith, hope, and trust, assured of God's forgiveness and tender understanding, we can turn away from that which has brought us so much anguish. We don't have to carry our regrets and feelings of guilt with us.

MILDRED TENGBOM, *GRIEF FOR A SEASON*

Chapter 5:

WHEN FRUSTRATION COMES TO CALL

When we talk about frustration, we generally mean those feelings brought about by shocking changes in our worldly circumstances. Loss of property, loss of a job, disappointed expectations. These events, and so many others, leave us feeling frustrated and helpless. "How could this happen to me?" *we ask.* "Who did this to me?"

The hard lesson is that even though the events that led to our frustration just came out of nowhere, the solution will not. It's up to us to quit trying to figure out how this happened and turn our attention to what we can do about it. Frustration leaves us feeling out of control, prey to random forces. When frustrated, we must learn to seek out the areas we can control and learn to accept that the ultimate controller of our circumstances is always watching out for us.

WHEN ONE DOOR CLOSES, ANOTHER OPENS

Two days before the 1993 Malibu fire destroyed their home, Duane and Lucile brought their contributions of blankets, clothes, and household items to their church to share with those who had lost their homes in the devastating Laguna Beach fire days before. The couple was surprised and pleased to receive an award in worship that Sunday, honoring their years of dedicated Christian service. Their joy continued as they celebrated Lucile's birthday on Monday. "We knew ourselves to be truly blessed," Duane says.

Tuesday morning, election day, dawned hot with Santa Ana winds. Lucile left early for jury duty in another city. As Duane sat at his computer, he received a telephone call from a friend. "Turn on your television. There's a wildfire burning in your area, and it looks to me like it's coming up the hill behind your house." Duane looked out the window, stunned, and saw fire on the horizon from right to left. After a few thwarted minutes trying to save his house, he gave up and evacuated as his neighbors had already done. Duane barely had time to grab a few belongings before he saw the fire right outside his yard. As he drove his car out of the neighborhood toward safety, firefighters saw a fireball explode inside his attic. The house went up in flames.

For several hours, Duane and Lucile were unable to get in touch with each other; they had no certain news about their home. After they were reunited hours later, they drove to a polling place outside their area and obtained special permission to vote, since their own polling place was in the fire zone. "There was nothing we could do but wait to find out what

> *ℬut we have this treasure in jars of clay to show that this all-surpassing power is from God and not from us. We are hard pressed on every side, but not crushed; perplexed, but not in despair; persecuted, but not abandoned; struck down, but not destroyed.*
>
> *2 Corinthians 4:7–10 NIV*

had happened to our home," Lucile explains. "Why miss an opportunity to vote?"

They stayed in a motel that night and prayed together: "God, whatever it is, give us the strength to handle it."

When they saw their home late the following afternoon, all that was left was a chimney and a tiled shower stall standing on a naked concrete slab. Flames 1,500 degrees hot had demolished everything else. Duane relates, "We knew that what was important was that we were both alive and well."

As they searched through the rubble of what had been a beautiful home, they discovered a stack of forks fused together in a twisted lump, all that remained of their silver service for 12. Their extensive collection of rare bibles, all their art and treasures from a lifetime of travel to other countries had disappeared into the ruins. A few dishes had somehow survived, though the dishwasher in which they once sat was melted to nothing.

Sifting through the ashes, Lucile somehow found her engagement ring, which had been in a drawer on the now nonexistent second story of

their home. "It struck me that the only posses-
sions that were left from our 50 years of marriage were in Laguna Beach, hopefully being
used by persons who needed them."

"We thought of all our years of memories,"
Lucile recalls. "And we knew that even if we
didn't have the material evidence of our life
together, we still had our memories." Believing
that "when one door closes, another opens,"
the couple decided to take the opportunity to
move to a retirement community and start a
new life there. Five years later, Lucile
remembers, "We never shed tears over our
house. There was no despair or depression. We
both knew that if people just turn to God for
comfort and strength and trust Him, everything
is easier."

Life certainly changed for Duane and Lucile on
that autumn day when fire engulfed their home,
but they never lost track of the fact that what
didn't change was most important: God's loving
presence through it all, the good and the bad,
the closed and open doors.

Have you ever known a weakening in the inward places of your soul because you had let slip the memory of what God did in the past? You had believed His words, you had sung His praises, for in very truth you had seen His words fulfilled. And then, somehow the memory faded, blotted out by disappointment....
May the Lord, by His Spirit, quicken our memories...

AMY CARMICHAEL, *EDGES OF HIS WAYS*

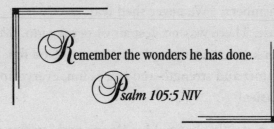

*R*emember the wonders he has done.

*P*salm 105:5 NIV

Only he who gives thanks for the little things receives the big things.

DIETRICH BONHOEFFER, *LIFE TOGETHER*

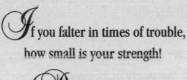

If you falter in times of trouble,
how small is your strength!

Proverbs 24:10 NIV

UPS AND DOWNS:
THE WHOLE PICTURE

Help me understand, O God, that we can't have
good without bad—a head without a tail. Help
me remember the joy when grief strikes my
heart. For just as it takes a negative to create a
photograph, it takes dark and light to complete
creation. Therein lies the promise: Darkness is
only half of the portrait of life.

Open our eyes, dear Lord,
That we may see
The far vast reaches of eternity.
Help us to look beyond life's little cares
So prone to fret us

And the grief that wears
Our courage thin.
O may we tune our hearts
To Thy great harmony
That all the parts may ever be
In perfect, sweet accord.
Give us Thine own clear vision, blessed Lord.

CORRIE TEN BOOM, *EACH NEW DAY*

EASING BACK

When moments like these overwhelm, help us find even small ways to regain a sense of holding the reins to what happens next. Control is as elusive as clutching an ice cube.

Call to me and I will answer you, and will tell you great and hidden things that you have not known.

Jeremiah 33:3 NRSV

Man was made for Joy & Woe;
And when this we rightly know
Thro' the World we safely go,
Joy & Woe are woven fine,
A Clothing for the Soul divine.

WILLIAM BLAKE, "AUGURIES OF INNOCENCE"

THERE *IS* SOMETHING TO BE DONE

I blew it. Again. O Lord, help me know that wringing my hands in the wake of failure is as useless as lamenting storm-felled trees. Give me eyes to see beyond chaos to possibilities. In that way, I won't miss finding out what could happen if I picked up a saw and took to that tree, making firewood around which friends can gather.

Lord, when my soul is weary
and my heart is tired and sore,
and I have that failing feeling
that I can't take any more;

then let me know the freshening
found in simple, childlike prayer,
when the kneeling soul knows surely
that a listening Lord is there.

RUTH BELL GRAHAM,
SITTING BY MY LAUGHING FIRE...

OUT WITH THE OLD FAVORITES

The familiar is disappearing from neighborhood and nature, and we grieve the loss. Yet, we're resurrection people, unafraid of endings because of the promise of beginnings. On the other hand, we must learn restraint: Help us to temper our actions with wisdom.

Sing away sorrow, cast away care.

MIGUEL DE CERVANTES SAAVEDRA, *DON QUIXOTE DE LA MANCHA*

GOOD AND BAD NEWS:
NOTHING STAYS THE SAME

Just when I settle in with one reality, something
new disrupts. Overnight change, God of all the
time in the world, is comforting and grief-
making, for it's a reminder that nothing stays
the same. Not tough times, not good ones
either. Despite today's annoyance, I'm grateful
for change, assured it will take me to new
moments you have in mind.

*We aspire to the top to look for Rest; it lies at
the bottom. Water rests only when it gets to the
lowest place. So do men.*

**HENRY DRUMMOND, *THE GREATEST THING
IN THE WORLD***

*I have instructed you to follow me
What way I go;
The road is hard, and stony—as I know;
Uphill it climbs, and from the crushing heat*

No shelter will be found
Save in my shadow: wherefore follow me;
the footprints of my feet
Will be distinct and clear;
However trodden on, they will not disappear.

EDNA ST. VINCENT MILLAY,
"JESUS TO HIS DISCIPLES"

DARING TO WONDER

Why, O God, do bad things happen? Can my anger that they do be a prayer? It's all I have to offer. I find relief sharing it with you; for now, that's all I need.

Put the good of your life in the progressive
freedom of your mind, freedom from all the
illusions of the flesh, and in the improvement
of your love for your fellow man . . . you will
be aware of a joyous sensation full of liberty
and happiness. You will be surprised to see
that the same external conditions, with which

*you were concerned...will not prevent the
coming of the greatest possible happiness.*

LEO TOLSTOY, *THE LAW OF LOVE
AND THE LAW OF VIOLENCE*

TIME TO GROW UP

Pete and Clara were stunned when their
financial adviser counseled them to declare
bankruptcy. For a number of years, Pete's career
had been on the rise; he was the golden boy of
his firm. At the same time Clara's work as a tex-
tile artist was more and more appreciated. As
things got better and better, their life expanded
to include a large home in an exclusive neighborhood, two luxury cars, vacations, and a full
round of entertaining with other up-and-coming
young professionals. Their discovery that Clara
was pregnant only added to their belief that life
was absolutely perfect.

And then, two months before the baby was due,
Pete's job was eliminated. Their bank accounts
would be closed; their charge cards cancelled
and rendered useless.

"We had been playing house like children," Clara admits. "If there was money to spend, we spent it, never bothering to save for the future. It all seemed so perfect, we didn't look at the fact that things at Pete's work weren't going so well. Suddenly, we were broke."

Bankruptcy was only the beginning. The big house had to be sold, the cars exchanged for more practical vehicles with lower monthly payments. It took Pete several months of job hunting before he found a position with a less prestigious firm at half the salary.

"And in the midst of all of this," Pete recalls, "we were still excited about the baby. That really kept us going. I didn't have a job, there was no money, the future seemed uncertain. But we were going to have a baby, and that mattered more than all the other stuff."

Little Angelica is now three years old and the apple of her parents' eyes. She has never lived in a fancy house or ridden in luxury cars. All she knows is that she has a mom and dad who love her and come home from work each day to pick her up from her grandmother's house.

"Our previous life—when everything seemed so perfect and we had plenty of money—seems so unfocused now. So what if we have to scrimp and save? We know what's really important: to be together as a family, to show our love to each other, to work once a month at a homeless shelter—something I would never have dreamed of doing before," Clara asserts. "That's what really counts."

Therefore we do not lose heart. Though outwardly we are wasting away, yet inwardly we are being renewed day by day. For our light and momentary troubles are achieving for us an eternal glory that far outweighs them all. So we fix our eyes not on what is seen, but on what is unseen. For what is seen is temporary, but what is unseen is eternal.

2 Corinthians 4:16–18 NIV

Are you tired? Worn out? Burned out on religion? Come to me. Get away with me and you'll recover your life. I'll show you how to take a real rest. Walk with me and work with me—watch how I do it. Learn the unforced rhythms of grace. I won't lay anything heavy or ill-fitting on you. Keep company with me and you'll learn to live freely and lightly.

JESUS, MATTHEW 11:28, *THE MESSAGE*

GETTING IN THE LAST WORD

Knee-deep in our home's disaster-ravaged left-overs, we weep and wail, knowing it's okay to mourn, for "stuff" is the log of our lives. Yet, with the hearts of rebuilders, we'll not let disaster have the last word.

There is no sorrow, Lord, too light
To bring in prayer to Thee;
There is no anxious care too slight
To wake Thy sympathy.

Thou, who hast trod the thorny road,
Wilt share each small distress;
The love which bore the greater load
Will not refuse the less.

There is no secret sigh we breathe
But meets Thine ear divine;
And every cross grows light beneath,
The shadow, Lord, of Thine.

JANE CREWDSON, "THERE IS NO SORROW,
LORD, TOO LIGHT"

I BLEW IT . . . AGAIN

Rejection. A foul word—overpowering when it happens to me. Help me not to overreact when my effort doesn't succeed. Next time it could.

> Those of steadfast mind you keep in peace—in peace because they trust in you.
>
> *Isaiah 26:3 NRSV*

TALK IS CHEAP

Promises, empty promises, politics to pulpit to people around the table. I'm numbed by how easily we don't mean what we say. God help me to be consistent.

There are so many conflicts and hostilities in this place lately, Lord, one almost has to duck. There are so many feuds and suspicions. It is as if poison had been released in the air. . . . Let your compassion, your forgiveness, your tremendous understanding begin to stir in everyone, deeply, strongly, rising up with such power it destroys every vestige of spite and unkindness . . .

MARJORIE HOLMES, *WHO AM I, GOD?*

SHRINK, SHRANK, SHRUNK

Pay cuts and wage freezes have come as a shock, Lord, and I'm working harder for less.

Help me learn to balance not just the checkbook but my consumer appetites as well, so I can decide what's really important, in both lean and fat times.

Prosperity is not without many fears and distastes; and adversity is not without comforts and hopes.

FRANCIS BACON, "OF ADVERSITY"

OVERWHELMED WITH NO DIRECTION TO GO

Defeat has stopped me in my tracks. I see no options, no possibilities. Yet paralyzing doubt can be relieved by finding something to believe in, something as simple as dandelions, rainbows, dawn, thunder and lightning. God will find me there.

I have said this to you, so that in me
you may have peace. In the world you face
persecution. But take courage: I have
conquered the world!

John 16:33 NRSV

GETTING "UNSTUCK"

As she opened her birthday cards, Jeannine felt a pang of failure. By the time she reached 45, she had expected to be in a very different stage of life. Ten years ago, Jeannine had hoped to be happily married, financially successful, and reasonably satisfied with her life. Yet here she was divorced once, in an unhappy relationship she was not even sure was healthy, stuck in a dead-end job she'd had for 12 years. It was time to take stock.

Easier, of course, would have been to remain in the job, the relationship, the lifestyle she had carved out for herself. Doug told her every day how wonderful she was; so why did his

occasional bursts of temper leave her feeling
unsettled and unlovable? Was it normal to have
moments of fearing the man with whom you
lived? And why was she so reluctant to make a
marriage commitment?

When she had begun her job as a legal secretary,
she had seen it as a stepping stone to her own
career as an attorney. There had always been
some reason why she hadn't started law school,
though, and at her age, it now seemed a ridicu-
lous idea. How could she pay for law school on
her salary? With house and car payments, she
barely made ends meet as it was.

Was there anyone to blame? Jeannine thought
of all the years she had prayed to meet the
"right man." God certainly hadn't kept the
divine part of that bargain. Ouch, she thought,
realizing that in a bargain, both parties make a
promise to do something. She let herself look
more closely at this idea. Truth be told, all these
years, she had spent more time complaining
than actively working to make the desired
changes in her life. Every time she thought
about leaving Doug or searching for a new job,
fear and inertia had stopped her progress.

From that day on, Jeannine prayed differently. "God, let me be ready for the new life you have in store for me." She wasn't sure exactly how that prayer would work, but it felt right. And, as she prayed it day by day, she felt something inside her change, too. When Doug came at her in one of his rages, she stood firm and refused to let him push her around. It wasn't long before she ended what she could now see was an abusive relationship.

She started looking at her job differently, too. Sure, it was security but it was also unrewarding and unchallenging. She wanted more from her life. Jeannine took the plunge of selling her home and moving to a small apartment in another town so she could look for meaningful work without the burden of a large mortgage.

Jeannine found a church home, joined a women's support group, took classes at a nearby community college. She made changes in her life little by little but was still caught by surprise when her forty-sixth birthday rolled around. This time, as she opened her cards, she felt blessed by the love she felt from family and friends. She realized that even though "Mr. Right" still had not come to call, she felt better about herself than she had in years. Through her work at a legal assistance center for immigrants, she was really making a difference in others' lives. She loved her little apartment and new group of friends. The old dreams of law school, the fancy house, latest car, and perfect marriage seemed unimportant now. Jeannine's prayers had been answered; her new life was hers to enjoy.

Why, O Lord, do you stand far off?
Why do you hide yourself in times of trouble?

David, Psalm 10:1 NIV

Give me heart-touch with all that live,
And strength to speak my word;
But if that denied me, give
The strength to live unheard.

Edwin Markham, "Supplication"

Yet, in the maddening maze of things,
And tossed by storm and flood,
To one fixed trust my spirit clings;
I know that God is good!

JOHN GREENLEAF WHITTIER,
"THE ETERNAL GOODNESS"

ALL ARE WELCOME

Sticks and stones of prejudice feel like they're breaking bones. Yet God calls us by name, numbers the hairs on our heads, guards our comings in and goings out, lifts us to high places and sets angels over us. How can we doubt our value with such overwhelming evidence to the contrary!

I praise You for Your sovereignty over the broad events of my life and over the details. With You, nothing is accidental, nothing is incidental, and no experience is wasted. You

hold in Your own power my breath of life and
all my destiny. And every trial that You allow
to happen is a platform on which You reveal
Yourself, showing Your love and power, both
to me and to others looking on.

RUTH MYERS, *31 DAYS OF PRAISE*

*B*ut they that wait upon the Lord shall
renew their strength. They shall mount up with
wings like eagles; they shall run and not be
weary; they shall walk and not faint.

*I*saiah 40:31 TLB

INCOMPLETE

"Incomplete" is stamped all over my life, Lord,
for I can't get everything done. Help me learn to
separate what can be finished from what can't,
giving to today only today's measure of tasks.

"O dreary life," we cry, "O dreary life!"
And still the generations of the birds
Sing through our sighing, and the flocks
and herds
Serenely live while we are keeping strife

ELIZABETH BARRETT BROWNING, "PATIENCE TAUGHT BY NATURE"

GATHERING STRENGTH IN SILENCE

The world is a noisy place. From family to office to leisure and routes in between, the air vibrates with ear-grabbing, relentless chatter. I yearn for quiet conversations with the God of still, small voices. My spirit, like my body, is easily bruised by too much noise.

Chapter 6:

SEEKING
YOUR ANGELS

*We're seldom, if ever, truly "in this alone."
In the midst of trouble, we may feel dread-
fully isolated, but healing rarely comes
without a little or a lot of help from outside, from those people in our lives who act
as our earthly guardian angels extending
God's help and love.*

*Seeking your personal angels might literally
mean going out and looking for the right
person to help with your particular problem. Just as often, though, it means learn-
ing to recognize the angels already
knocking at your door. Pain and sorrow
can blind us to the compassionate friends
nearby who are eager and able to help us
on the road to recovery. If you're ready to
seek healing, take a good look around.
Your earthly angel might be standing right
in front of you.*

FROM OUT OF THE BLUE, MARIE

When my daughter died, I had no desire to live, either. Lots of people sent cards, of course, and offered to help, but talking about her death just made me feel worse. I didn't return phone calls and basically isolated myself. My life as a single parent was over, and I could see no new life in sight."

A shadow passes over her face as June remembers a time that, though it happened years ago, seems like yesterday.

"Amy and I had only recently moved to a new community when she was diagnosed with leukemia. I did not have time to get to know new people; it took all my energy just to care for her and deal with the medical stuff. So when she died, all of my support system—my parents, brother, and a childhood friend—were far away, but I needed to keep my job in the place where Amy had died. I was alone. All I could do was pray that God would somehow help me through this, the hardest thing I had to face in my life.

"The week after Amy died, I received a card from a woman who had read of Amy's death. The next week, she sent another card and a short note. The week after that, she wrote a longer letter saying she was thinking about me. From then on, as regular as clockwork, Marie's letters arrived every Wednesday. It got so that I looked forward to her letters. In a life that was shattered and had so little substance, I could count on Marie."

Remember what Christ taught and let his words enrich your lives and make you wise; teach them to each other and sing them out in psalms and hymns and spiritual songs, singing to the Lord with thankful hearts.

Colossians 3:16 TLB

Marie asked nothing of June. She offered her presence through letters but did not push to get together. Each letter ended, "I pray for you each day. Call if you need anything. Love and under-

> For he will command his angels
> concerning you to guard you in all your
> ways. On their hands they will bear you up,
> so that you will not dash your foot against
> a stone.
>
> *Psalm 91:11–12 NRSV*

standing, Marie." In this nonthreatening way, June felt cared for but not intruded upon. When she felt stronger several months into the one-way correspondence, June called Marie and they finally met.

"I don't know what I had expected but Marie surprised me. She wasn't the color, shape, age, or size I had thought she was, so we had a good laugh about that," June says. "If I had met her before all this happened, I don't know if we would have struck up a friendship, but after months of receiving her lovely letters, I felt like I knew her well. Once we actually met, we began to do things together—museum days, dinner, going out to a movie. She introduced me to her family and friends and they all sort of adopted me. It wasn't long before I felt like I belonged in a place I thought I'd always hate, since it was where Amy died.

"Marie laughs when I say she saved my life but it's true," she continues. "Her letters brought me back to life, or at least helped me find a new life without Amy. Life will never be the same, of course, but now I have the strength to go on, thanks to a friendship that would never have happened if Amy hadn't died."

SURPRISED BY A VISIT

How lonely we are when trouble strikes. Send us a sign, Lord. We long for a message, a hand reaching toward us. And just as God promised, we're visited by a Presence in dream and day-light revelations, and we are grateful for God's personal, one-on-one caring.

THANKING AND DOING:
A PACKAGE DEAL

I remember those who gave, sometimes at great
effort,
  time,
  energy,
  money,
  information,
  for me.
In their life-giving style, I'll spend myself for
others.

*Having Him plus the pain is infinitely better
than being without both.*

NANCY GROOM, *MARRIED WITHOUT MASKS*

Carry each other's burdens, and in this
way you will fulfill the law of Christ.

Galatians 6:2 NIV

COMPANIONS THROUGH
THE VALLEY

Watching how others have coped with what's troubling us now, we take heart from their creativity, Lord, knowing you will inspire us, too, to find innovative ways to move on.

Heavenly Father, we admit that the horizons of our world are pretty small Help us to expand our horizons by developing a concern for others. Direct our thoughts beyond our walls so that we may care about the whole world. We pray in the name of Jesus our Lord. Amen.

DONNA L. GLAZIER, *HEAVEN HELP ME*

HAND IN HAND

Angels are as close as an outstretched hand, tending us in illness, worry, and dark despair. They reach for us as hands of support beneath our elbows; as hands binding up; as hands holding ours; as hands patting shoulders in encouragement and applauding efforts made toward recovery. And, when it comes to that, in hands waving us on to the distant shore where a welcoming Creator waits.

The most powerful stimulant my soul can receive is an assurance, produced somehow, that it is at one with the Divine Life, and the best way for it to retain that assurance is by making other souls aware of their oneness with the Divine Life; of their inherent longing to be as God obviously meant them to be.

LLOYD C. DOUGLAS, *THE LIVING FAITH*

If you want to comfort others, let God first comfort you, and then share that comfort. But keep in mind that comfort is more than "sympathy." Our English word comfort *comes*

from two Latin words that together mean "with strength." The Greek word Paul used means "to come alongside to help." Our word encouragement *means "to put heart into." In other words, we comfort people, not by unanswerable arguments, but by unfailing love and acceptance.*

WARREN WIERSBE,
WHY US? WHEN BAD THINGS HAPPEN TO
GOD'S PEOPLE

Where you go I will go, and where you stay I will stay. Your people will be my people and your God will be my God.

Ruth to Naomi, Ruth 1:16 NIV

SMALL BUT MIGHTY MESSENGERS

When trouble strikes, we're restored by the smallest gestures from God's ambassadors: friends, random kindnesses, shared pain and

support, even a stranger's outstretched hand.
And we get the message: God cares.

Teach me to feel another's woe,
To hide the fault I see;
That mercy I to others show,
That mercy show to me.

ALEXANDER POPE, "AN ESSAY ON MAN"

SCANNING THE HORIZON

When hope seems gone, I spy doves like those
God sent Noah to assure him the storm was
subsiding. Doves of inspiration, knowledge, and
understanding; doves in the shape of those not
letting me travel alone. I'm energized for the
rest of the journey. Land is in sight.

THANK-YOU NOTE

Gentle healers of mind, body, and spirit are
surely a gift from you sent to travel lonely roads
as our companions. Sustain them as they sustain
us; they are a channel of your love.

Sweet souls around us watch us still,
Press nearer to our side;
Into our thoughts, into our prayers,
With gentle helpings glide.

HARRIET BEECHER STOWE

UNLIKELY ANGELS

Belgian priest Henri Nouwen left his teaching
position at Harvard to live with and be pastor to mentally impaired people who, with the
help of others caring for them on a daily basis,
are able to live in a community rather than be
confined to a mental institution. Nouwen wrote
about how some of these people had touched
his life:

"There is a man who lives in my community who asks me, 'What are you doing here?' every time I see him, and a woman who smiles and says 'Welcome!' whenever I see her. I could regard these people as mentally handicapped, or I could see them as angels who are bringing me important messages every day—to ask myself what I'm doing with my life on earth, and to remind me that I am welcome here."

Mother wanted her life to count for God in a way that touched other people. So she reached out to those whom she knew were hurting inside as much as she was. She started a fellowship group for widows. Together they lunched, together they laughed, and together they cried. One dear widow said recently, "What did we ever do before your mother became a part of our congregation?"

PEG RANKIN, *YET WILL I TRUST HIM*

> *J*onathan became one in spirit with David, and he loved him as himself. . . . And Jonathan made a covenant with David because he loved him as himself. Jonathan took off the robe he was wearing and gave it to David, along with his tunic, and even his sword, his bow and his belt.
>
> *1 Samuel 18:1, 3–4 NIV*

ANGEL BLOSSOMS

Overwhelmed, we're greeted by God's springtime messengers as daffodils rise from their winter sleep, relieving our doubts with the promise of new blooms.

LEARNING THE WAYS OF COMFORT

No class today; the teacher's sick
I think of her, I make it quick.
Who sits with her, drops by her home;
Or cares that she is quite alone?

Potato soup I've cooked and seasoned,
There is plenty made, and yet, I reason,
She's surely friends a hundred-fold,
   Enough to care, to share her load.
I'll make no call
But could it be she's quite alone?
   I lift the phone.

To bear one another's burdens is a privilege,
as long as we remember that the Lord is the
final person to carry the load.

DALE EVANS ROGERS, *GRANDPARENTS CAN*

One man gave me great encouragement
because he was so genuine—and I sensed he
was willing to "tough it out" with me. I read
and reread these lines from his letter:

"Never in my life have I had to contemplate
the loss of one I love as much. I know how
difficult a time it is for you, and it's a real test
of my faith. To me, faith means not trying to

*'understand' things like this. Faith is just
knowing God's love is supreme..."*

**Elizabeth Dean Burnham,
When Your Friend Is Dying**

Up Close and Personal

O God of doves and rainbows, we know what
hope looks like as family, advocates, friends,
and those who've shared similar fates
accompany us through this dark tunnel of crisis.
Behind these faces, we recognize yours.

*As we tune in to God, He tunes us in to
people.*

Betty Malz, Women in Tune

*A potent way in which hope manifests itself is
when you as a caregiver let people know by*

your words or actions that you are willing to help them struggle through their problems. Your consistent, caring presence with them through thick and thin instills hope. The knowledge and expectation that another person will be with them during difficult times provides people with a sense of security.

KENNETH C. HAUGK, *CHRISTIAN CAREGIVING—A WAY OF LIFE*

... listening can be a greater service than speaking.

DIETRICH BONHOEFFER, *LIFE TOGETHER*

. . . he brings us alongside someone else who is going through hard times so that we can be there for that person just as God was there for us.

2 Corinthians 1:4, The Message

THE POWER OF A VOICE

Who was my sorrow for
last week when from my mud-room door
I watched an arrogant mallard drake,
From a wintering-over flock of eight,
Fly to my lawn from a nearby lake.
He stumbled, injured,
Right leg strong, left folding down.
I watched that green-headed, curly-tailed
drake
Hesitate. Then, heeding a hen's loud call,
He hobbled to corn scattered near a garden
wall.
Oh, God, I am injured, too
My sorrows slow to mend.
But today, as I turned from the mud-room
door
Came the call of a faithful friend.

ON THE WINGS OF OTHERS

We recognize your angelic messengers in the welcoming support and open-handed suggestions of others willing to share how we, too, can learn to live in the new ways that illness or trouble sometimes dictates. We see your hand in the clever, creative, and determined adaptations they pass on to us and are carried as if by a thousand lifting wings.

HELPING HANDS

Beneath supporting hands of friends and helpers, we feel God's strong grasp and hold on, no longer alone.

THROUGH THE VALLEY

When life seems impossible, they appear—mentors, role models—teaching us how to walk boldly as people of light rather than as those hiding in darkness.

I have noticed that when one who has not suffered draws near to one in pain there is rarely much power to help. . . . Does pain accepted and endured . . . create that sympathy which can lay itself alongside the need, feeling it as though it were personal? . . .

AMY CARMICHAEL, *ROSE FROM BRIER*

If loneliness is your problem, make it a priority in your Christian service to start solving loneliness for somebody else. . . . Put yourself out for this person, not in an ostentatious way that makes him feel embarrassed and patronized, but in a sincere desire to form a good relationship.

In such an atmosphere of self-giving love, loneliness—crippling, corrosive loneliness— simply cannot survive.

JOHN HAGGAI, *WIN OVER LONELINESS*

STAYING NEARBY

I can do it myself, I protest, but, O God, I know it's not true. Open me to your limitless love found in the skillful caring of those who know firsthand my present trouble. They bring your message home and I feel you close, as close as angel wings beating gently upon my stubborn loneliness.

Rejoice with those who rejoice; mourn with those who mourn.

Romans 12:15 NIV

These loving people most likely do not know it, but right now they are the structure which causes my life to go on. They have become me, for a little while, and they carry on my days until I can catch up with it all.

PAULA D'ARCY, *SONG FOR SARAH*

*E*ach one of us needs to look after
the good of the people around us, asking
ourselves, "How can I help?" That's exactly
what Jesus did. He didn't make it easy for
himself by avoiding people's troubles,
but waded right in and helped out. "I took
on the troubles of the troubled" is the way
Scripture puts it.

*R*omans 15:2–3, The Message

*. . . the dark clouds of depression are moving;
they do pass. One of the most helpful things
we can do for a friend at such a time is to
stand by him in quiet confidence, and assure
him this, too, shall pass. . . . If he discovers that
our concern for him is genuine, then the quiet
assertion of our own confidence in God's
continuing care and concern for him will
assist tremendously in his recovery.*

GRANGER E. WESTBERG, *GOOD GRIEF*

ONE IS THE LONELIEST NUMBER

When trouble strikes, it can be gentled by
accepting comfort instead of going it alone.

*It was but the last time when I saw my father
that he told me, with an ejaculation of gratitude
to the Giver of every good and every perfect
gift, that in all the vicissitudes of his fortunes,
through all the good report and evil report of
the world, in all his struggles and in all his sorrows, the affectionate participation and cheering encouragement of his wife had been his
never-failing support, without which he was
sure he should never have lived through them.*

JOHN QUINCY ADAMS

A HEALING NIGHT

Exhausted from walking this troubling road,
we're intercepted by those who care. Knowing
God is as close as a prayerful thought and

they're as near as a phone, we feel care spread like wings over us, and we can finally sleep.

Have we trials and temptations?
Is there trouble anywhere?
We should never be discouraged,
Take it to the Lord in prayer.
Can we find a friend so faithful
Who will all our sorrows share?
Jesus knows our every weakness,
Take it to the Lord in prayer.

JOSEPH M. SCRIVEN, "WHAT A FRIEND
WE HAVE IN JESUS"

FLYING IN FORMATION

We're tempted to give up until we see the geese. God provided them a "V" in which to fly, a main "point" goose providing wind resistance for followers. Geese take turns, take up slack, in the natural rhythm of things. When we ask for help, we let someone else take the point position. And we feel an updraft of air to rest in, and feel God in this current of wind.

*Two are better than one . . .
For if they fall, one will lift up the other . . .*
Ecclesiastes 4:9–10 NRSV

One day a little girl slipped into her father's study. Without saying a word, she sat quietly on the floor close beside him, watching him at work. After a while he said, "Honey, is there something you want?" "No," she replied, "I'm just sitting here loving you."

MILLIE STAMM, *BE STILL AND KNOW*

Chapter 7:

WHAT IS GAINED?

So what's the point of it all? Why does God allow us to suffer pain, illness, loss? The answers to these questions will probably never be revealed to us in this life. But when we take stock of our experiences, the good and the bad, we find that the dark times have left us with more than just unpleasant memories. Perhaps we have gained new insights into our own personalities, found strength and depth we never knew we had.

And what do we do with these emotional gains? We may go on to lead richer, more enlightened lives. We may also seek to comfort those who hurt as we have hurt, thus heeding God's call to look after our fellow humans. Is this perhaps why God has permitted suffering in our lives? We can't answer that question. But our lack of sure knowledge should not stop us from trying to act as God's tools for good here on earth.

Wisdom in a Dream

Sarah could hear a voice whimpering, faintly, just beyond sleep. *The dream,* she realized, *here comes the dream again.* Of course it was her own voice whimpering, protesting, pushing against the feelings the dream always stirred up, the way the wind pushes litter from the side of the road and lifts it spinning into the air. Then she heard another voice, soothing, reminding her that even nightmares are intended to bring healing and urging her to trust her mind.

"Let it come," Sarah told herself. Like Ebenezer Scrooge reaching out to the third and final Christmas spirit, she assented, "I trust that where this dream takes me, I need to go."

The spiders came. They had been coming to her in her sleep for as long as she could remember. They had been coming more often since she had found a skilled and compassionate professional to share them with.

"Tell me about the dreams," the therapist had said, appearing interested. It was she who introduced the possibility that though terrifying, they were gifts from Sarah's soul, promising release, recovery, healing. So she spoke aloud the night-mares that had been haunting her sleep. And she began to risk speaking about the violence that had haunted her childhood.

For a long time it seemed to Sarah that she had opened the trapdoor to hell and fallen in. The pain came with a force that took her breath away. Some days it was all she could do to just breathe. It was a Herculean effort to simply function, stay alive, get up, eat, sleep, talk; it all seemed too much. She felt like she was drown-ing in the flood of memories.

Then you will know the truth, and the truth will set you free.

John 8:32 NIV

Every time she let go of another memory, it was followed by 10 more, and then more; it seemed unending. The memories emerged through her senses: smells, tastes, sensations, hearing voices, seeing things she knew weren't there. She feared she was losing her mind. The reality was that she was not losing it, she was finding it.

As this happened, Sarah's constant headaches ceased. Her anxiety, the nervousness that used to come in waves, out of nowhere, calmed. For 10 years she had had chronic sore throats, inflamed tonsils so painful she could not swallow. Now her tonsils became quiet, pain-free. She learned she could trust herself when she disciplined her children—fair, firm, and never hurtful. They became more secure as she became more confident.

She discovered her anger, and like a toddler in the terrible twos, she claimed the right to experiment with the word "no." She found the word worked like a key, unlocking the door to free-

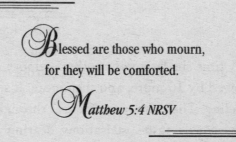

Blessed are those who mourn,
for they will be comforted.

Matthew 5:4 NRSV

dom. On the other side of the door Sarah discovered "yes." Her relationships became richer and more satisfying.

One morning Sarah woke up and braced herself for the inevitable familiar dread, despair, and exhaustion to sweep through her. But it did not. She scanned herself, like a computer checking for viruses. Usually she found numerous ones and would have to begin the grueling process of dissecting them until they finally disintegrated. For the first time, the scan came back, "safe."

She noticed she was breathing from a different part of her body, full deep breaths. Her muscles were loose and her hands and feet were warm. "Safe," it kept flashing in her head. She turned over and buried her head in her husband's chest and they both cried. She had made it out of hell.

So why was the nightmare returning? She was disappointed. The spiders were everywhere, webs upon webs covered the walls, huge spiders dangling from them busily spinning. An enormous spider suddenly dropped from the ceiling in front of her face. She started to scream, but it spoke: "Be still and listen!"

The spider continued in a firm but tender voice, "You have yet to thank us for all the work we have done for you." Then she knew: They had been weaving together the memories. They had been spinning threads connecting the past to the present, where her wounds could be treated and healed.

The spider smiled and then began to transform itself. As Sarah watched, its legs folded and then became two wings. Before her now was a shimmering red butterfly with enormous eyes. It flew up and landed on her chest, on top of her heart. She felt its energy flowing through her body with every beat.

I've been driven many times to my knees by the overwhelming conviction that I had nowhere else to go.

ABRAHAM LINCOLN

FILLING UP THE EMPTY SPACES

When violence strikes us like mud splashed from a puddle, we bolt our doors and cover our heads. God can draw us from hiding and nudge us to get busy. For violence, like water in a puddle, can only thrive in a hole. Inspired, we can fill it up with hands that, instead of wringing helplessly, are busy rebuilding.

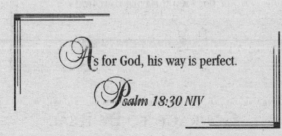

As for God, his way is perfect.

Psalm 18:30 NIV

It is inhuman to wall yourself up in pain and memories as if in a prison. Suffering must open us to others. It must not cause us to reject them.... God chooses to suffer in order to better understand man.

ELIE WIESEL, *GATES OF THE FOREST*

Do not fear, for I have redeemed you;
I have called you by name, you are mine.
When you pass through the waters, I will
be with you; and through the rivers, they
shall not overwhelm you; when you walk
through fire you shall not be burned,
and the flame shall not consume you.
For I am the Lord your God.

Isaiah 43:1–3 NRSV

COURAGE TO BE REAL

Help me understand, Lord, that the courage I
am praying for is not dry-eyed stoicism and
perky denial. Courage is not hiding my feelings,
even from you, and putting on a brave false
face. Rather it is facing facts, weighing options,
and moving ahead. No need to waste precious
time pretending.

TAKING A SECOND LOOK

When things go wrong, God is usually the first we blame. Forgive us for even considering that you would deliberately hurt one of your very own children. For what could you possibly have to gain? Thank you for your presence; forgive our easy blame of you.

His is a loving, tender hand, full of sympathy and compassion.

DWIGHT L. MOODY, *ANECDOTES AND ILLUSTRATIONS*

NEVER TOO LATE

Regardless of what the future holds, I'm savoring all sorts of wondrous things I've been too busy to notice before. A thousand daily marvels bring a smile to my face. Through your grace, Lord, rather than thinking how sad it is that I missed them before, I'm delighted to be seeing, doing them now. These small wonders energize me, and for that I'm thankful. It's never too late to be a joyful explorer.

"Hope" is the thing with feathers
That perches in the soul,
And sings the tune without the words,
And never stops at all,

And sweetest in the Gale is heard;
And sore must be the storm
That could abash the little Bird
That kept so many warm.

I've heard it in the chillest land,
And on the strangest Sea;
Yet, never, in Extremity,
It asked a crumb of Me.

EMILY DICKINSON, (254)

> *D*o not repay anyone evil for evil.... Live
> at peace with everyone. Do not take revenge,
> my friends, but leave room for God's
> wrath.... If your enemy is hungry, feed him; if
> he is thirsty, give him something to drink.
>
> *R*omans 12:17–20

WHAT MATTERS MOST

No matter how broken my life, God can create
something new from the pieces, like a quilt
made of scraps, leftovers of a better time but
warming nonetheless.

*Even the worst of life-experiences can be used
to achieve the best of life's response.*

EDGAR N. JACKSON, *WHEN SOMEONE DIES*

Someone is there, I realized. Someone is watching life as it unfolds on this planet. More, Someone is there who loves me. It was a startling feeling of wild hope, a feeling so new and overwhelming that it seemed fully worth risking my life on.

PHILIP YANCEY, *DISAPPOINTMENT WITH GOD*

*T*his plan of mine is not what you would work out, neither are my thoughts the same as yours! For just as the heavens are higher than the earth, so are my ways higher than yours, and my thoughts than yours.

*I*saiah 55:8–9 TLB

WHAT A DIFFERENCE A KINDNESS MAKES

Kindness sows a seed within me that begins to sprout where before all was barren. Leaves of trust start to bud, and I branch out. I take in gentle caring and loving nudging and realize I might just go ahead and bloom! After all, God arranged spring after winter.

We remember all too well the bitter discoveries we have made when we have tried to run our lives our own way, when we try to steer our own craft. Wilt Thou come aboard, Lord Jesus, and set us on a true course.

PETER MARSHALL, *THE PRAYERS OF*
PETER MARSHALL

GETTING BACK

They had been coworkers for 20 years, close friends for 16 years, business partners for two years, and enemies for 15 months. What a waste of time. That's what it boiled down to at this point: a colossal waste of time.

Of course, it was also a waste of money. Roger cringed just approaching the figures in his mind.

He had never totaled exactly how much he had lost; he was afraid if he made it that clear he'd have to hurt Jim, pummel his face, cause physical harm. The feelings were so out of character, so unfamiliar, so intensely overwhelming, Roger decided he had better just avoid it.

Roger hated feeling this way. His rage was eating away at him. He found himself snapping at people he loved, being impatient. He was especially frustrated with all the bills. He couldn't get himself to pay them without wanting to throw them across the room. They felt like little reminders of Jim's betrayal, his thieving, tearing down all he had worked so hard to build.

Roger had not understood the depth of Jim's gambling problem or he would never have entrusted him with so much. He knew Jim liked to bet; heck, he had even accompanied him to the track on weekends. He had not recognized the signs of an addiction out of control, and it was too late now. There was nothing left but debt, Jim's debt, but in reality their joint obligation. Roger had consulted an attorney and discovered that although it was unfortunate, legally, he was liable.

It took a year to untangle the whole mess, but finally he was making headway. He had to go to work for a competitor, a competitor he had been beating. They were happy to have him on their team; he resented being there.

> *D*o not let your hearts be troubled.
> Believe in God, believe also in me. In my
> Father's house there are many dwelling places.
> If it were not so, would I have told you that I go
> to prepare a place for you? And if I go and
> prepare a place for you, I will come again and
> will take you to myself, so that where I am,
> there you may be also.
>
> *J*ohn 14:1–3 NRSV

Roger lost track of Jim. Once the attorneys had finally sorted out who would pay for what and how and when, he had decided to wipe Jim off the face of the earth, at least in his mind. In another year he would finally be free of the financial burden Jim had created. But still it didn't matter; his anger kept building.

Then one day he answered the phone and heard Jim's wife on the line, crying. "I've left Jim," she announced, as if it mattered to Roger. "I'm divorcing him."

> *I* know what it is to be in need, and I know what it is to have plenty. I have learned the secret of being content in any and every situation.
>
> *Paul, Philippians 4:12 NIV*

Roger didn't know what to say; he felt ill. "There's no one else I can turn to; we have no friends left," she continued, "You were always like an uncle to the kids, please, do you think you can help us?"

"What do you want?" he asked, angry. "I have no money left, you know that."

He was surprised by her answer, "I want my kids to know you, to know that there was a time when their dad was healthy and had friends of your caliber. They need to know that, especially Jimmy."

Roger hung up the phone and went for a walk. He found himself at the deli where he and Jim used to eat lunch. They had shared their dreams, their hopes, their worries, as they outlined their plan to start their own business. It had been brilliant; it really had. It would have been very successful. Tears stung Roger's eyes. He walked on. He found himself praying, nothing formal, just talking inside his head.

He walked by the junior high school. He stood there thinking about his son, and Jim's son. His own son was going to be okay. The past year and a half had been very hard on his family, but it was getting better. He felt his anger coalescing, transforming from liquid to solid, like the gelatin figures his daughter liked to eat.

A couple of years ago he had taken a bible study course at church on forgiveness. He thought it would be naive, a class on turning the other cheek. The nun had surprised him.

"Enabling evil, ignoring sin, is not forgiveness," she had explained. "Sometimes simply healing the hurt in you they have caused is forgiveness enough; you are releasing them from the consequences of their actions, and that is a great gift." Yes, that was forgiveness. He was clearing up the debt Jim created and wounded him with; perhaps that was forgiveness enough?

Roger found himself back at his home, hand on the phone.

"Hello?" Jim's wife's voice on the other end of the line startled him, even though he had placed the call. He heard a voice, his own voice, saying, "I'm calling you back because I've been thinking. Why don't I pick Jimmy up on Saturday, and I'll take the boys to lunch and to see a game. Tell Jimmy I'll be there at 11:30. Tell Jimmy I'll be there."

He had found another way of forgiving, even of loving his enemy; he would help to heal the children.

Our only task is to keep in step with him. He chooses the direction and leads the way. As we walk step by step with him, we soon discover that we have lost the crushing burden of needing to take care of ourselves and get our own way, and we discover that the burden is indeed light. We come into the joyful, simple life of hearing and obeying.

RICHARD FOSTER, *FREEDOM OF SIMPLICITY*

TWO-PART INTENTION

Confession without lament is not honest; our grief is evidence of trust in God.

More things are wrought by prayer
Than this world dreams of.
Wherefore, let thy voice
Rise like a fountain for me night and day.
For what are men better than sheep or goats
That nourish a blind life without the brain,

If, knowing God, they lift not hands of prayer
Both for themselves and those who call them
    friend?
For so the whole round earth is every way
Bound by gold chains about the feet of God.

ALFRED, LORD TENNYSON,
"MORTE D'ARTHUR"

Trust in the Lord with all your heart
and lean not on your own understanding;
in all your ways acknowledge him,
and he will make your paths straight.

Proverbs 3:5–6 NIV

CHOOSING HOPE

Like a speed bump in the drive-through, a decision lies in our path, placed there by God to remind us hope is a choice. Choosing to live as people of hope is not to diminish or belittle pain and suffering or lie about evil's reality. Rather it is to cling to God's promise that He will make all things new.

You cannot control every circumstance, but you can respond to each one in faith.

ELLIS MORRISON, *LIFE HURTS—GOD HEALS!*

"THANKS FOR THE CARD, GARRISON KEILLOR"

My dying friend received a postcard
That was caring and succinct.
He wrote of a 21st birthday gift for his
    daughter,
A jacket. White. A squirt gun filled with
    disappearing ink.

Flying to Copenhagen,
    As other passengers slept,
        He spoke with a pen.

He was sorry she was ill.
Sorry she could not attend his Denver gig.
It wouldn't be much of one without her, he
    ribbed.

My friend's pale day was splattered with joy.
One brilliant, indelible ink hit.
Life is never simply tragic.
We find the magic if we watch for it.

AMAZING GAINS

Just when all seems hopeless, prayer lifts us like a wave on the ocean. A sturdy craft, prayer doesn't hide from pain, but uses it like the force of the sea to move us to a new place of insight, patience, courage, and sympathy. Always, it is God's hand beneath the surface holding us up.

I still struggle and do not expect to find all the
answers to the multitude of questions which
perplex my soul. My certainties have been

*few; my doubts have been many. Yet the
bedrock assurance which has held my feet
from slipping is the confidence that God loves
me and nothing occurs outside of His
providential control.*

JAMES E. MEANS, *A TEARFUL CELEBRATION*

*H*e will wipe away all tears from their
eyes, and there shall be no more death,
nor sorrow, nor crying, nor pain.
All of that has gone forever.

Revelation 21:4 TLB

*I know not what the future hath
    Of marvel or surprise,
Assured alone that life and death
    His mercy underlies.
And if my heart and flesh are weak
    To bear an untried pain
The bruised reed He will not break,
    But strengthen and sustain.
. . . I know not where His islands lift*

Their fronded palms in air;
I only know I cannot drift
Beyond His love and care.

JOHN GREENLEAF WHITTIER,
"THE ETERNAL GOODNESS"

GOING STRAIGHT TO THE PUNCH LINE

As we face worrisome days, restore our funny bones, Lord. Humor helps rebuild and heal, sparking hope and igniting energy with which to combat stress, ease grief, and provide direction.

What strength do I have,
that I should still hope?
What prospects, that I should be patient?

Job, Job 6:11 NIV

After Job had prayed for his friends, the Lord made him prosperous again and gave him twice as much as he had before.

Job 42:10 NIV

BELOVED CHILDREN OF A LOVING PARENT

In self-doubting times, we can rely on God as a loving parent who wills wholeness for each child—known and tended personally.

God moves in a mysterious way
  His wonders to perform
He plants his footsteps in the sea
  And rides upon the storm.
Deep in unfathomable mines
  Of never-failing skill
He treasures up his bright designs,
  And works his sovereign will.

Ye fearful saints fresh courage take;
The clouds ye so much dread
Are big with mercy, and shall break
In blessings on your head.

WILLIAM COWPER, "LIGHT SHINING
OUT OF DARKNESS"

FROM A TINY SEED, BLOOM

With God's hand tending it, even the tiniest seed
of hope cannot be dislodged.

In our finiteness, we must continually drop to
our faces before God in worship, saying, I
bow before You as one of Your creatures.
Thank You that, while I cannot understand
everything, my hand is held by the eternal, all-
wise, Infinite God, the Creator.

EDITH SCHAEFFER, *AFFLICTION*

ACKNOWLEDGMENTS:

Publications International, Ltd., has made every effort to locate the owners of all copyrighted material to obtain permission to use the selections that appear in this book. Any errors or omissions are unintentional; corrections, if necessary, will be made in future editions.

Page 11: Excerpt from "Felicity of Grief" by Edna St. Vincent Millay. From *Collected Poems,* HarperCollins. Copyright © 1954, 1982 by Norma Millay Ellis. All rights reserved. Reprinted by permission of Elizabeth Barnett, literary executor.

Pages 22, 97: Reprinted from *The Collected Verse of Edgar A. Guest.* Copyright © 1984. Used with permission by NTC/Contemporary Publishing Group.

Pages 24, 56: Excerpts from *He Cares, He Comforts,* by Corrie ten Boom. Copyright © 1977. Reprinted with permission from Fleming H. Revell, a division of Baker Book House Company.

Pages 26, 160: Reprinted from *Song for Sarah* by Paula D'Arcy. Copyright © 1995. Used by permission of Harold Shaw Publishers, Wheaton, IL 60189.

Pages 30, 70, 177: Excerpts from *The Prayers of Peter Marshall* edited by Catherine Marshall. Copyright © 1954. Reprinted with permission from Chosen Books, Inc., a division of Baker Book House Company.

Pages 52, 81–82, 152: Excerpts from *Yet Will I Trust Him,* by Peg Rankin. Copyright © 1980. Regal Books, Ventura, CA 93003. Used by permission.

Page 71: Reprinted from *Listen to the Green* by Luci Shaw, copyright © 1971. Used by permission of Harold Shaw Publishers, Wheaton, IL 60189.

Page 84: Excerpt taken from *All the Days* by Vance Havner. Copyright © 1976. Reprinted with permission from Fleming H. Revell, a division of Baker Book House Company.

Page 93, 132: From *Who Am I, God?* by Marjorie Holmes. Copyright © 1970, 1971 by Marjorie Holmes Mighell. Used by permission of Doubleday, a division of Bantam Doubleday Dell Publishing Group, Inc.

Page 93: Excerpted from *Mothering by Heart,* by Robin Jones Gunn. Multnomah Publishers, Inc. copyright © 1966, by Robin Jones Gunn.

Pages 94, 123–124: From *Sitting by My Laughing Fire...,* by Ruth Bell Graham. Copyright © 1977, by Ruth Bell Graham. Used with permission from the author.